HAUNTED ONTARIO 3

HAUNTED ONTARIO 3

Ghostly Historic Sites, Inns, and Miracles

TERRY BOYLE

DUNDURN
TORONTO

Photo Credits: St. Thomas Cemetery photos courtesy of Paul Blisson. All others are the property of Terry Boyle.

Editor: Laura Harris
Design: Jesse Hooper
Printer: Webcom

Library and Archives Canada Cataloguing in Publication

Boyle, Terry, author
      Ghostly historic sites, inns, and miracles / Terry Boyle.

(Haunted Ontario ; 3)
Issued in print and electronic formats.
ISBN 978-1-4597-1765-7 (pbk.).--ISBN 978-1-4597-1767-1 (epub).--ISBN 978-1-4597-1766-4 (pdf)

      1. Haunted places--Ontario. 2. Haunted hotels--Ontario. I. Title. II. Series: Boyle, Terry. Haunted Ontario; 3.

BF1472.C3B69 2014   133.109713   C2013-908376-6
                                                                              C2013-908377-4

1   2   3   4   5   18   17   16   15   14

We acknowledge the support of the **Canada Council for the Arts** and the **Ontario Arts Council** for our publishing program. We also acknowledge the financial support of the **Government of Canada** through the **Canada Book Fund** and **Livres Canada Books**, and the **Government of Ontario** through the **Ontario Book Publishing Tax Credit** and the **Ontario Media Development Corporation**.

Care has been taken to trace the ownership of copyright material used in this book. The author and the publisher welcome any information enabling them to rectify any references or credits in subsequent editions.

J. Kirk Howard, President

The publisher is not responsible for websites or their content unless they are owned by the publisher.

Printed and bound in Canada.

VISIT US AT
Dundurn.com | *@dundurnpress* | *Facebook.com/dundurnpress* | *Pinterest.com/dundurnpress*

Dundurn	Gazelle Book Services Limited	Dundurn
3 Church Street, Suite 500	White Cross Mills	2250 Military Road
Toronto, Ontario, Canada	High Town, Lancaster, England	Tonawanda, NY
M5E 1M2	L41 4XS	U.S.A. 14150

I dedicate this book to my grandson, Talon Douglas-Cates

Contents

An Examination of Hauntings

DO GHOSTS AND SPIRITS EXIST? MY ANSWER WOULD BE "YES." FOR THE past thirty-nine years, I have interviewed countless people, from all walks of life, who have shared their inexplicable experiences with me. For them these occurrences are real. There may not be any understanding of the meaning of some of the experiences, but they did happen to them. When I research a book on a haunting, I *always* visit the locale where the event has happened and I interview the people at the site. Occasionally, I experience some form of unusual activity during the investigation. When I meet people they often ask me two major questions: What got you interested in ghosts, and could you explain this area of study?

I always insist that I can only share what I have observed. I have no definitive answers, only theories and comments.

When I was a child I would often hear knocking sounds or faint whispers in the air. I was not alone! Someone or something was near me.

This visitation would cause me to scream in the night. My mother would always come to comfort me. She probably thought it was just my vivid imagination, but I knew differently.

In the beginning of my adulthood, I began a career as an investigative journalist. I had chosen this field of study in order to explore the world of history and to write books. I have never wavered from this direction. At first I wrote books about Ontario history, such as *Under This Roof*, *Old Homesteads of Ontario*, *Ontario Memories*, *Teachings from the Longhouse*, and *Ontario Album*. During the course of my research into our historical past, people would share their other-worldly experiences. It usually would start with a ghost story about a residence or a chance encounter on a country road with an apparition. I would listen to the stories and invariably be reminded of my childhood experiences.

What was really happening and why were so many people having these unusual experiences that seemed connected to them or to the place? The questions continued and I finally realized that I needed to apply my skills as a journalist and find some answers.

It began with *Haunted Ontario*, a collection of thirteen true stories of encounters with the spirit world. I knew in my heart that I was meant to continue my journey writing about this subject, loosely known as parapsychology. The Oxford Dictionary definition of parapsychology states, "The study of mental phenomena outside the sphere of ordinary psychology, e.g. hypnosis, telepathy etc." Some people believe the origins of parapsychology research commenced on February 20, 1882, when the Society for Psychical Research (SPR) was officially constituted in England. According to the textbook written by Harvey J. Irwin and Caroline A. Watt, and used in a course on Parapsychology at the University of Edinburgh entitled, Introduction to Parapsychology, "Parapsychology is the scientific study of experiences which, if they are as they seem to be, are, in principal, outside the realm of human capabilities as presently conceived by conventional scientists. Thus parapsychological phenomena ostensibly indicate the operation of factors currently unknown to, or unrecognized by, orthodox science, popularly referred to as paranormal factors."

The Society for Psychical Research was founded principally on the initiative of some academics at Cambridge University and associates, all of whom believed that various claims for the existence of paranormal phenomena warranted scientific scrutiny. Irwin and Watt stated, "Recorded experiences, of course, may be found among all cultures and in all historic periods. Two main factors can be seen to have led to the foundation of parapsychology in 1882. These were the movements known respectively as Mesmerism and Spiritualism."

Mesmerism was founded by Franz Anton Mesmer, who was born in Switzerland in 1773 and later studied medicine at the University of Vienna. Mesmer was interested in studying how physicians could exert an influence over their patients.

Irwin and Watt add, "At the folk level there was a tradition that certain divinely inspired individuals had the power to cure the sick by touch, the so called 'laying on of hands.' Some of these healers used magnets to strengthen the healing force that purportedly emanated from them [the hands]."

Eventually Mesmer discovered that the use of a magnet was not necessary. The healing effect could be achieved with any object which had passed his hands. He concluded that there existed a healing force, or 'fluid,' known as animal magnetism (so named to distinguish it from ordinary mineral magnetism). It was discovered that as Mesmer made magnetic passes over his patients they would fall into a sleep-like state or trance.

Irwin and Watt stated, "In this state, the 'magnetized' individuals would be remarkably compliant with Mesmer's suggestions, reporting, for example, complete freedom from pain."

There were also other reported by-products of magnetic induction known as "higher phenomena." Some patients suddenly had the ability to see events that were sensorily inaccessible. Mesmer used this technique to evoke telepathy, clairvoyance, travelling clairvoyance, the expression of transporting clairvoyant awareness to a distant location and other parapsychological experiences.

A number of years ago I interviewed a professional nurse who had experienced time travel. Her story began at an archaeological dig that took place near Collingwood, Ontario. Someone had discovered the site of an ancient Native village. Her husband was associated with the archaeologist at the site and they decided to visit the dig. When they arrived at the site, she encountered time travel.

She suddenly found herself as a young woman sitting in a circle of Native elders, including a medicine man. She also saw that she lived in the village near this medicine man. She was close with this holy man and appeared to have been happy.

She was married to a young Native who was killed in battle. This medicine man knew this was going to happen, but did nothing to prevent it. She had discovered this and had come to hate the medicine man.

Then suddenly, she was back in the present with her husband. He was aware that something had happened to her. She did not want to leave the area. She knew she could return to that time at any moment.

Two years later, she had a deep yearning to return to the site. Her husband had died and she had too many unanswered questions. She followed the same pathway to the spot where she had stepped back in time. Once she arrived in the same location she received a strong message instructing her not to go back.

Her questions were, "What do I do with this experience? What does it all mean?"

Where does one go with questions like that! Was this "travelling clairvoyance"?

This force that Mesmer talked about applies also to the story in this book entitled "A Scent of Roses." In this story people travel to a farm in Marmora, Ontario to experience the miracle of divine healing by the laying of hands, the drinking holy water, or by the power of prayer.

Although Mesmerism was a forerunner of parapsychology, the Society for Psychical Research was on a different path. They set about establishing a religious movement entitled Spiritualism.

The Spiritualism movement originated in America in the middle of the nineteenth century; it was brought to public awareness by events recorded in the Fox household.

Irwin and Watt wrote about the beginning of this spiritual movement. "In December 1847, a blacksmith named John Fox, his wife, and two of their children, fourteen-year-old Maggie and twelve-year-old Kate, moved into a rented, wooden cottage in Hydesville (Rochester), New York. The house was said to have had a reputation for being associated with uncanny events, and in the latter half of March, 1848, the family began to hear a variety of strange sounds — rapping, bangs, and scrapings — as if furniture was being shifted."

John Fox thought the window sashes were being rattled by the wind. So he carefully checked all the windows in the house, giving each one a firm shake. His daughter, Kate, observed that each time her father shook the windows the noises were heard, as if in reply.

"It occurred to Kate to snap her fingers to see if that would elicit a similar response. The 'ghost', as it was taken to be, responded to this challenge with raps in the pattern.

"Eventually, word got out about the ghost in the Fox home. More and more people flocked to the house to witness the communications."

The Fox sisters began to travel across the country demonstrating how they could communicate with the spirit world.

The sisters held séances and participants often felt the touch of an invisible hand. Objects moved unaccountably and musical instruments playing without human intervention. The sisters enjoyed success as mediums for many years.

The Fox sisters had captured the imagination of the American public. Irwin and Watt add, "Mediums sprang up in other parts of New York State, and by the early 1850s, followers of spiritualism in New York City numbered in the tens of thousands."

In the next few years, spiritualism had spread throughout America and to Europe.

In a book entitled *Ghosts and Spirits*, by Chambers Harrap Publishers, it was stated, "By 1888 alcoholism was taking its toll on both Kate and Maggie. Their sister Leah had given up managing her two younger sisters. While the two sisters were at this low ebb, a reporter offered $15,000 to Maggie and Kate for an exposé of their methods.

"On the night of 21 October, 1888, Maggie performed at the New York Academy of Music, with Kate in the audience. Maggie showed how a simple cracking of the joints of her toes could produce a sound loud enough to be heard through the whole theatre. This had been put forward as a possible explanation for the rapping sounds, but no one had been able to prove it until this admission was made."

In 1889, Maggie retracted her confession and returned to doing séances.

Kate and Maggie died as paupers. The Fox home was dismantled and moved to Lily Dale, in New York State.

The spiritualist community of Lily Dale was created in 1879, as a home for mediums. Lily Dale is located about an hour drive southwest of Buffalo. It is a settlement comprised of a cluster of nineteenth-century, gingerbread houses. Today there are forty mediums living in Lily Dale.

Every year approximately 22,000 people visit Lily Dale to participate in classes and workshops, to share public church services, mediumship demonstrations, and lectures, and to have private appointments with mediums.

We went to Lily Dale to ask Greg Kehn to assist us in seeking out the spirits in the Orillia Opera House. It was incredible to work with Greg. He is truly a gifted medium and is able to see the spirit world and communicate messages. Historical facts verified almost every spirit he encountered in the Orillia Opera House.

Although the story about the Fox sisters ignited a spiritualist move-ment, it was not the first such paranormal story to make history in North America. The "Baldoon Mysteries" story in this book was an earlier event — and a sensational happening in the community of Baldoon, Ontario.

That story concerns the McDonald family, who were persecuted for three years by the curse of a witch. The family not only experienced knocking, but a host of other paranormal occurrences.

What is a "ghost"? The Oxford Dictionary states, "The supposed apparition of the dead."

Renowned author Dr. Hans Holzer was one of the world's foremost experts on the subject of the paranormal and authored more than one hundred books on parapsychology.

According to Dr. Holzer, he believed there was a difference between a ghost and a spirit. "A ghost appears to be a surviving emotional mem-ory of someone who has died traumatically, and usually tragically, but is unaware of his or her death. A few ghosts may realize that they are dead but may be confused as to where they are, or why they do not feel quite the way they once did."

Dr. Holzer believed that when death occurred unexpectedly or unac-countably, or when a person died who lived in a place for a very long time and was attached to the premises, there would be shock, trauma, and an unwillingness to part with the physical world.

Holzer stated, "Ghosts — individuals unaware of their own passing or incapable of accepting the transition because of unfinished business — will make themselves known to the living people at infrequent intervals."

This could be the case in some of the hauntings at Black Creek Pioneer Village.

Dr. Holzer points out that in his research "no more than 10–15 percent of all sightings or other phenomena are 'real ghosts'. The larger portion of all sightings or sound phenomena is caused by a replaying of a past emotional event, one that has somehow been left behind, impressed into the atmosphere of the place or house." (See the "Cherry Hill House" story in this book.)

Dr. Holzer mentions his view of the difference between a ghost and spirit. He believes ghosts do not travel or follow people home; neither do they appear at more than one place. Reports of apparitions of the deceased are not ghosts to Dr. Holzer, but free spirits.

He defines a spirit as such: "Spirits are people like you and I who have passed on to the next world without too much difficulty or too many problems. They are not bound to anything left behind in the physical world. They do, however, have ties and emotional interests in the family or friends they left behind."

Holzer believes that spirits are people who have died and are living in their duplicate "inner body," the etheric body. They are different from the physical living people in respect to certain limitations and the time element, but spirits are simply people who have passed on to the next world with their memories and interests intact.

Whether a ghost or spirit, people of all walks of life have had encounters with these unusual entities. An older man, who had taken my historical, haunted walking tour of Bala, Ontario, shared this incredible experience with me: Four years ago, on the night of his birthday, he retired to bed. Sometime in the night a spirit visited him. She appeared by his bedside. He was unable to make out her features, but she leaned over and whispered in his ear. He could not make out what she was saying; then she looked at him again and vanished. He wondered who she was, why she came, and what she had said.

He believed it was his mother. Now here's the twist! He had been adopted as a baby and never met his real mother. He believed his mother had been unable to find him while she was still alive, but had continued the search for him in death — and had found him.

On his next birthday, he wondered if this female spirit would return.

In the middle of the night she reappeared. Again, she attempted to whisper something in his ear. This time, she moved to the end of the bed and gazed at him. He knew it was her. He called out to her, "Mother!" and she shattered like broken glass and vanished!

The experience left him feeling loved. It was the closure he needed in his life. Although she never returned, he knew it had been her.

Some people ask about poltergeists.

Chambers stated, "Poltergeist-related phenomena can involve objects seeming to move with no cause, including heavy items such as furniture, as well as smaller items; bangs, knocking and rapping noises; thrown objects, which sometimes follow an unusual trajectory, or seem to be aimed at a specific person; rains of small objects such as stones or coins, sometimes falling inside a house; foul smells; spontaneous fires, sometimes breaking out on walls or ceilings; electrical disturbances, including the switching on and off of lights and appliances; the levitation of either objects or people; and the manifestation of liquids such as blood, water, or oil."

A few years ago, a group of actors were on stage rehearsing a play in the Gravenhurst Opera House. One of the actors suddenly felt something dripping onto their shoulder. Almost immediately, they were soaked and a small puddle had formed on the stage floor. It was blood! Rehearsal stopped. A ladder was used to climb up into the ceiling area of the stage, to see if there was a wounded animal up there. They found no trace of blood or any animal in the ceiling. It was an unnerving event.

I have discovered over the years that numerous theories abound when it comes to explaining the existence of ghosts, spirits, or any form of paranormal activity. I do not suggest that I have found the answers, but I continue to explore this fascinating world of the paranormal. I truly love listening to people's stories and visiting the sites where the activity is occurring or has occurred. In each event or story, I approach the subject matter objectively. *Haunted Ontario 3* has been a joy to explore, investigate, and write. I hope you enjoy reading the book as much as I enjoyed writing it.

Terry Boyle
Burk's Falls, Ontario, 2013

Black Creek Pioneer Village, Toronto

WE DO MANY THINGS TO PRESERVE AND PRESENT HISTORY. THERE ARE libraries, museums, heritage homes, and open-air living history sites, to name a few. A living history site consists of a collection of buildings that represent life as it was in a particular era and location. Historical interpreters, often dressed in costumes reflecting the styles of the period, bring energy and a sense of community to these places.

Imagine the energy imprint that is created from a collection of buildings brought together from a moderately large area representing skills, customs, and lifestyles. Now imagine the potential attachment to buildings and businesses that were considered good examples of their purpose and time. Attachment could infer "haunting."

These buildings may or may not have had any historical connection to one another; so that would mean that ghosts unfamiliar with each other, but brought together, could create an interesting atmosphere.

Next ask yourself what happens when you fill these buildings with interpreters, who are dressed for, and acting out the details of, the past.

Well I suggest you may have confused and, perhaps, angry or indignant ghosts. Let's check out such a village — Black Creek Pioneer Village — and see what's what.

The Stong Homestead

~ Black Creek Pioneer Village ~

Put salt on the doorstep of a new house so that no evil can enter

THE STONG HOMESTEAD MAY APPEAR UNINHABITED, BUT YOU WOULD be mistaken. Two spirits linger here, maintaining a connection between dimensions. There is a reason for this state of affairs, but what is it? Perhaps you, the reader, can visit this site and solve the mystery of why these spirits have a foot in two worlds.

Our story begins with Daniel Stong, born in Pennsylvania in 1791. His parents, Sylvester and Barbary, immigrated to Canada in 1800. During the War of 1812, Daniel served with a British regiment.

On January 23, 1816, Daniel married Elizabeth Fisher in the township of Vaughan. They soon settled on Lot 25, Concession 4, in West York. Daniel and Elizabeth constructed a sturdy, squared-log house that consisted of three small rooms and a large stone fireplace. The couple raised seven children in this small dwelling.

The need for a much larger home for his growing family prompted Daniel to begin construction of a two-storey, hand-hewn log home dressed with clapboard siding in 1832. Daniel built it directly behind the original log cabin. The home featured several bedrooms, a separate parlour, and a large, impressive kitchen with a brick fireplace and bake oven. Their eighth and final child was born in the new home.

Eventually Daniel acquired an additional one thousand acres around his existing property.

Tragedy struck the Stong family on September 7, 1845, when their eighteen-year-old son, Michael, was killed in a horrible hunting accident. It was an accidental shot and he subsequently died in the upstairs bedroom of the house. Michael became the first person to be buried in the cemetery on the Stong family farm.

Michael is one of the spirits who comes and goes in the house. The second spirit to be reported in the building is a woman. She has been seen sitting in a chair on the second floor. No one knows who she is. The Stongs did have two daughters, Mary and Catherine.

The image of a woman has reportedly been captured on film, but I was unable to locate it.

Nancy, a Black Creek Pioneer Village employee, has worked here since 1999. Nancy is one of those special individuals who are sensitive to the spirit realm. She can tune in to the frequency connecting the dimensions. Nancy shared some of her experiences with me.

The Stong House.

"During my first year, I heard strange noises. Creaking sounds, as if someone was walking upstairs. When I went to investigate there was no one there. I thought I was alone at the time.

"Then I heard about the unusual death of Michael Stong and the stories about the haunting."

Nancy began to suspect that the death of Michael and the unusual events in the house were related. Some activity has to do with the narrow piece of wood used as a window stop to keep the window propped open.

"Every once in a while, a window stopper resting on the window sill will fly off and land on the floor. This can happen with the upstairs or downstairs windows. If that happens I yell at Michael like a mother would, 'Hey Michael settle down.'"

"I have a policy that whenever a new person begins working in the house I never say anything about Michael."

Nami, another interpreter, recalled her first tour of duty in the Stong homestead.

"It was the fall, about closing time. It was cloudy and dark outside. I saw what I thought was the last person to come down the staircase from upstairs and leave the building. I was about to lock up the house when I suddenly heard footsteps upstairs. I clearly heard the footsteps. I first

The unpredictable window stop.

shouted out 'it's closing time', but never heard a reply. As I climbed the stairs to the second floor I called out. When I reached the second floor I walked around — but there was no one there. I was very scared. I later asked my boss if the house was haunted. My boss just laughed."

Catherine Crow, a historical researcher for special events and a ghost-tour guide who started the walks at Black Creek Pioneer Village at Halloween, believes Michael is a mischievous spirit who haunts his own bedroom on the second floor, and the kitchen on the main floor.

Catherine has spoken to several costumed interpreters who work at the village and had similar paranormal experiences in the Stong homestead. Here is what they had to say.

"One young interpreter reported hearing hollow-sounding footsteps coming from the boys' bedroom on the second floor when she was downstairs alone in the parlour. There was no one else in the house at the time except for Nancy, another costumed interpreter, who was busy working in the kitchen on the first floor. The young interpreter timidly went upstairs and found that all of the rooms were completely empty. She went back downstairs and told Nancy what she had heard. Nancy went upstairs and noted with surprise that the chain rope in the boys' bedroom was mysteriously swinging back and forth, on its own."

Stong House kitchen, where Michael moves items around.

"Nancy said, 'Michael, please stop that,' the chain rope suddenly stood still again."

Nancy has worked here for a long time and is quite familiar with Michael's antics.

Catherine added, "He'll often move things around in the kitchen, across the table or other work areas when she is working downstairs."

One staff member said Michael constantly moves a chair around upstairs. You can also hear someone playing Jacks.

Catherine shared a good story about getting locked inside the house.

"Another interpreter, Ivan, once conducted a tour of teenagers, about Michael's age, through the house. When they went to leave, they could not get the front door in the kitchen to open at all. The front wooden door is not very sturdy. Only a small iron latch keeps the thin door shut and the door will often blow open with a strong wind."

Ivan commented that it was as if a force was holding the door shut.

Catherine continued, "This went on for about fifteen minutes; the group interpreter was getting desperate and was about to get a student to crawl through one of the open kitchen windows to get help when the door suddenly and inexplicably opened ... on its own!

"Another interpreter received a response from Michael when she went to lock up for the night. She went upstairs to do a final check. She said she felt a strange presence beside her as she was about to head down the narrow stairs at the back of the house. She offhandedly said, 'Goodnight Michael.' She was halfway down the stairs when a knocking sound came from the top of the stairs behind her, as if Michael was saying goodnight."

One employee I spoke to indicated that the female spirit had been seen on several occasions. She also shared a remarkable event that happened one December 23 in the Stong house.

"I went into the parlour and gazed at the Christmas tree on display. Then I felt a little tug on the back of my dress. When I turned around the tugging stopped. I looked back at the tree and the antique ornaments started to spin around. This lasted for a few seconds and then stopped."

Nancy later shared an incredible experience with me concerning a direct descendant of the Stong family: an elderly woman, nearing her nineties, appeared one day at the Stong house. She declared herself to be the great-great-granddaughter of Daniel Stong. She wanted to sit in her old bedroom for a few minutes. She proceeded to do just that. Sometime later she returned and said to Nancy that her deceased mother came to her and talked with her for half an hour. The lady died two weeks later!

Maybe that's the woman spirit detected in the house; or, is there an opening here to the other dimensions. As for Michael, do you suppose he chooses to stay or perhaps he does not know that he could move on?

Black Creek Pioneer Village Cemetery

Whippoorwills call for the souls of the dead

YEARS AGO, I WAS PRESENTING A LECTURE ON THE PARANORMAL IN Collingwood, Ontario. A man seated in the audience raised his hand to speak. He told a tale about one incredible encounter with the spirit world in a cemetery.

He was attending the funeral of his uncle in Madoc, Ontario. The community is in a rural setting and was predominately settled by the Irish and the Scots.

After his uncle was buried he decided to remain at the cemetery. He sat down with his back against a tree. He was still there at twilight. Many people believe that twilight is the time when the veil between dimensions is at its thinnest. It is a time to communicate with the spirit world.

Suddenly the man heard voices. Looking about, he was unable to see anyone in the graveyard. In disbelief he sat and listened intently to the sound. He soon realized the voices he was hearing were speaking in a foreign tongue. Then he recognized the language — it was Gaelic.

Could it be that the dead still commune with one another?

Black Creek Pioneer Village cemetery may not be any different. The graveyard is located beside the Fisherville Church, at the back of the village.

The church, built in 1856, originally stood in the old community of Fisherville, once located at Steeles Avenue and Dufferin Street. It was moved in 1960 and replaced the log church that once stood on the corner of the Stong farm.

The cemetery is original to the site. It was in use from 1845 to the 1920s, and is the final resting place for members of several local founding families, including Daniel, Elizabeth, and Michael Stong, and the Kaisers, the Hoovers, and the Boyntons.

Catherine Crow highlighted the cemetery haunting during a visit to Black Creek.

"At night, security employees at the village have reported seeing unexplained orbs of light in the cemetery on more than one occasion. At times these strange orbs have been seen outside the cemetery, floating over the dirt road in front of the church. These mysterious orbs are known to dance around in the air and weave above the gravestones."

There are many theories related to orb sightings. Some people believe they may be spirits, others think orbs could be portals or openings from one dimension to another. Other people believe that orbs are just specks of dust.

Over the years, hundreds of people have travelled to Ghost Road on Scugog Island near the community of Port Perry, Ontario, to see a mysterious orb of light that haunts a somewhat deserted side road. People claim to believe the orb of light is the spirit of a dead headless motorcycle rider. According to local lore the biker lost control of the motorcycle and was decapitated by a barbed-wire fence.

In 1986, six Niagara College film students arrived at the Ghost Road to do a short documentary about the story. Their aim was to capture the orb of light on film. The first night out everyone prepared for the arrival of the floating ball of light. One student was stationed in the field at the south end of the road where the rider supposedly hit the fence. They claimed a sphere of light the size of a basketball popped out of thin air and hovered in mid-air, sixty feet above them, for a few seconds.

The students managed to photograph and video tape the light. The photograph depicted the fuzzy outline of a human figure bathed in a strong white light. The video showed a more defined figure in the orb. The outing was a complete success.

So, back to Black Creek Pioneer Village — Animals often sense the presence of spirits. One night at Black Creek, a security employee brought a German shepherd guard dog with him on his night shift. Catherine elaborated:

"On the dirt road in front of the cemetery the dog became visibly agitated. He started to growl and bark. The dog then hunched down on all fours then rose up and started to back away from the area."

What had he seen or sensed?

Certainly, there have been full apparitions seen in this cemetery!

A "ghost boy" has been seen. He has been described as wearing nineteenth-century clothing. He appears frequently to tour guides and to visitors.

Catherine added, "The boy likes to join the back of tour groups for brief moments and then completely disappears.

"Sometimes, he isn't visible, but will tug on the clothes of an unsuspecting visitor or employee."

Cynthia, a tour guide in the village, told Catherine she saw the boy herself when she was approaching the church during a tour. Catherine continued, "As Cynthia was talking to her group on the road she noticed a small boy in a period outfit playing peek-a-boo with her from behind the back of the last visitor in line."

He was there one minute ... gone the next.

During the second annual ghost walk in October 2007, a young couple encountered the ghost boy and told Catherine about it.

"The young man told me he had a strange experience while walking back from the cemetery on the dirt road. He said he felt a persistent pulling and tugging sensation at the back of his jacket as they walked up the road. He asked his wife if she was grabbing his jacket. She told him that she was not touching him at all.

"This strange sensation continued until they reached the point where the road turns off by the mill and then the pulling and tugging on his jacket stopped all together."

If you are a "spirit-seeker" who isn't afraid of cemeteries, then perhaps a trip to the Black Creek Pioneer Village cemetery is just the ticket. Perhaps you have your own 'orb-theory' and share it with the tour guides.

The Richmond Hill Manse

~ Black Creek Pioneer Village ~

*Growing ivy on the outside of your house protects the inhabitants
from witchcraft and evil.*

IF YOU WANT TO BE WATCHED BY SOMEONE NOT OF THIS WORLD, BE
sure to visit the Richmond Hill Manse. The good reverend is waiting
for you.

The manse, located across from the church and cemetery at Black
Creek, was built in 1830. Originally situated at 88 Yonge Street in
Richmond Hill, the building — originally a private residence — became
a home for Presbyterian ministers in 1840.

During the 1970s, an official of the affiliated Presbyterian Church
found the manse too costly to maintain. The structure was designated as
an historical building and relocated to Black Creek Pioneer Village on
October 5, 1978.

The building itself represents what they call "plank-on-plank" construction, with wood planks stacked one on top of the other to create
six- to eight-inch walls. The construction technique was in vogue when

wood was cheap and plentiful. It provided an uneven surface for the application of plaster and stucco finishes.

In the early days, ministers would spend four to five years in a particular parish before moving on to the next church. Reverend James Dick preferred to stay put. In fact, he may have never left the manse at all! In life Reverend Dick occupied the building from 1849 until his death in 1885.

Reverend Dick had a reputation for being moody and eccentric. His uneasy energy remains in the building, and some employees are hesitant and nervous there.

Catherine Crow explained.

"'The manse gives off a disturbing vibe,' reported Curt, who works as a costume interpreter. 'I am too afraid to go upstairs.'"

He is not the first employee to sense the energy or spirit presence. Catherine added, "Harold is a volunteer at the village. His daughter was an employee at one time and she also worked in the manse, as a costume interpreter, until she requested a transfer to another building."

Harold described his daughter's apprehension. "She would actually sit outside the manse and only venture inside when she had to. She just found the atmosphere in the manse was too creepy. She felt like she was constantly being watched in the building by someone not of this world."

Richmond Hill Manse, circa 1830

Harold's daughter was not the only family member sensitive to the other side. Catherine explained, "Harold had a three-year-old niece who refused to step into the manse when he took her to the site. The three year old stood in the front doorway and said with a pout, 'mean man inside,' and then turned around and walked back up the pathway to the main road."

Ruthan Johnson, a former employee who worked for many years at Black Creek, had several glimpses into a world thought to have vanished a hundred years ago. When we met, Ruthan talked about the Richmond Hill Manse.

"In the minister's office, located on your left as you enter from the front door of the house, you can hear the books being pulled off the shelf; listen to the sound of turning pages. One employee would leave the Bible located in the office open to a certain passage. When he returned in the morning he observed that the Bible was open to a different passage.

"Occasionally you will hear coal being dumped in the parlour stove in the office."

It is not uncommon, early in the morning, for a staff member approaching the manse to witness someone peeking out through the curtains of the upstairs window. Sometimes people see a small infant running around the upstairs of the house. One time, when Ruthan was about to

In the Richmond Hill Manse office Bible pages are changed.

open up the church, she turned around to see the upstairs curtains of the manse house moving. There was no one in the house at the time.

The spirit of a little boy dressed in blue has been seen on a number of occasions in the house. Ruthan described him.

"The boy wears blue shorts, a white shirt, suspenders and a little jacket. He has blond hair and wears knee high socks. His clothing would date between the 1870s and 80s."

"He isn't afraid to appear to visitors at the village. He usually shows up when small children come through the house.

"At Christmas the boy dressed in blue enters the house through the front door. He then proceeds to the parlour and can be seen walking through the existing table in the house. Then he enters the downstairs bedroom situated by the staircase leading to the second floor. To your amazement you can actually see a dent in the bottom of the bed where he is sitting," said Ruthan.

A female employee was working in the Manse house alone one night during Christmas holidays. To her amazement, she saw the minister standing at the top of the stairs on the second floor. He appeared quite angry. The employee fled the building.

Ruthan mentioned that her husband Dennis, who also had worked at Black Creek, had actually seen the little boy.

Another employee at the manse heard a woman humming upstairs and the tiny footsteps of a child coming from the upper floor.

When Catherine was researching the ghost stories in the village, prior to the first Halloween ghost walk in 2006, she had decided to check out the manse for herself. This is what she discovered.

"Although the downstairs was nicely decorated with comfortable furniture it felt very depressing to me. It was on the second floor, however, that I encountered the angry presence spoken of by employees and visitors. I was on the second floor landing looking down the stairs. To my immediate right was a bedroom and from the doorway of this room I could literally feel hostile eyes boring into me, willing me to get out of the house. The longer I stood there the more intense the feeling became. I started shaking with fear and had to come downstairs."

A couple who arrived to take the ghost walk tour decided to walk to the site where the Manse house is located and this is what happened.

"The building intrigued them and they found an unlocked kitchen door and entered the house. They were standing in the kitchen when they heard distinct footsteps walking around upstairs.

"They assumed it was the caretaker for the village. They had seen him nearby, walking alone, just prior to their entering the building."

This was not the case.

"Much to the surprise of the couple, the caretaker walked in the front door of the manse while they were still standing in the kitchen — [he was] listening to the footsteps on the floor above. The couple asked the caretaker who was walking around upstairs since they had thought it was him. He said the second floor was closed to the public and was not in use that night and there should be no one upstairs. On further investigation he, in fact, found no one upstairs."

As if that wasn't enough, later that night a tour guide had her own experience with the spirits of the Manse house. Catherine explained, "One of the tour guides had finished her speech to her tour group in the manse and after everyone had left the house, she shut the front door and started up the main road with the group. She happened to look back at the building and saw a curtain in the front parlour being pulled back by an unseen hand, as if someone were watching to make sure everyone had finally left the area."

Rhona Hastings has visited Black Creek Pioneer Village on several occasions over the past forty years. She states, "I have always been drawn to a few of the houses. I don't call myself a psychic. I am just a little sensitive to things. I have a strong intuition.

"The minister's house I feel has energy. About sixteen years ago I went into this house and, as we all do when we visit the village, I looked around. It was a little unusual that there was no one in the house at the time telling the tale of the house or spinning the wheel as they do. I had a friend with me so I wasn't alone. We were looking in one of the rooms and turned our heads to the left where there stood an old lady smiling at me. She was very close to me. She was dressed with a long coat and a scarf [babushka] on her head. She stared at me and had a very warm smile. She actually looked like what I might look like as an old woman. My friend and I looked at one another and then looked back to the old woman and she was gone!"

Despite the apparent benevolence of the older woman who frequents the corridors of the manse, it would seem the reverend does not want you to overstay your welcome. So, as you enter the manse house I would suggest you take note of the time. The good reverend may, indeed, be watching over folks at the village — but it seems he is also keeping time and is happier once you're gone.

Roblin's Mill

~ Black Creek Pioneer Village ~

CANADIAN POET AL PURDY KNEW MORE THAN MOST PEOPLE ABOUT THE ghostly workers of Roblin's Mill. This excerpt from his poem, entitled "Roblin's Mill," sets the mood of this site:

> The lighting alters...
> and you can see...
> a bald man standing
> sturdily indignant..
> ....
> ....
> In the building men are still working
> thru sunlight and starlight and moonlight
> despite the black holes plunging down
> on their way to the roots of the earth

Built in 1842, the mill was originally located in Ameliasburg, near Belleville, Ontario.

Ameliasburg was once named Roblin's Mill, in honour of Owen Roblin, who had the mill built there.

Catherine Crow said, "Owen died at ninety-seven years of age, after the turn of the century. Will Roblin, Owen's grandson, took over ownership of the mill just prior to the First World War. He eventually lost interest in the mill and closed it down. Ameliasburg, without the mill, had a definite decline in commerce."

In 1964, the conservation authority acquired the mill and moved it to Black Creek Pioneer Village.

This five-storey stone building is powered entirely by a large, wooden overshot waterwheel. The mill machinery includes two runs of stones to grind wheat, lotting reels for sifting flour, and elevator belts to move grain and flour.

Roblin's Mill, 1842

Although there is not a sensational example of spirit activity in the building, Black Creek employees have believed for years that the mill is haunted by the "old ones."

Catherine alluded to one experience at the mill.

"Employees at the site have seen the big wheel turning when it has been disconnected for the winter, as if unseen hands were still going about the business of making flour." Other eerie phenomena and superstitions are also associated with the mill. For example, when pigeons [that roost in the mill's rafters] are restless and coo incessantly, a change in weather is believed to be on the way.

Poet Al Purdy may have gotten it right about the ghostly workers when he stated the following:

> Those old ones
> you can hear them
> lost in the fourth dimension
> what happened still happens
> a lump rises in your throat.

Burwick House

~ Black Creek Pioneer Village ~

*All windows should be opened at the moment of death
so that the soul can leave*

COME. DON'T BE AFRAID. OPEN THE DOOR AND ENTER. NOW CLOSE THE door. Turn around and embrace a world of unexplained occurrences that reach beyond your rational mind. In fact, just take one step beyond the veil of time and space and explore Burwick House at Black Creek Pioneer Village.

According to Catherine Crow, "The most famous and publicized spirits at Black Creek Village reside here, in Burwick House."

The home was built in 1844 in Burwick, Ontario (now Woodbridge). This dwelling, suitable for a country gentleman, is complete with fine furnishings made in Upper Canada and a selection of imports from Britain and the United States. A substantial stable and a landscaped yard and garden, reflect an owner with comfortable circumstances.

A number of staff members who have worked in the Burwick house have reported many cases of paranormal activity.

The Burwick House, 1844

Catherine stated, "Several members have reported unexplained activity, including knocking sounds, moving objects, hearing footsteps and feeling cold spots throughout the house."

"One young worker reported looking up from the kitchen table he was sitting at to see the dark shadow of a woman standing in the kitchen doorway. She [the shadow] disappeared shortly after that."

Another employee has claimed to have seen the same dark shadow of a woman on the central staircase.

In June of 2005, authors Maria da Silva and Andrew Hind highlighted the haunting of Burwick House in an article they wrote for *Fate Magazine*:

"It was late into the evening by the time Marlee and a co-worker began the short walk back to the administrative building after one of the park's nighttime events. Marlee found her eyes drawn towards the second floor of the building, where a pale white light illuminated one of the windows."

A staff member described the light as flickering, like a candle sputtering on its own wax. That employee thought someone might have forgotten to extinguish an oil lamp and decided to investigate.

"Pushing open the front door, Marlee and another employee felt an ominous presence that caused Marlee to pause in her steps. Regaining her composure, she began to climb the creaking stairs but her knees grew weaker with each step taken. She reached the landing, exhausted by the short ascent. There was no lamp burning, but Marlee suddenly caught sight of a black figure, a shadow that walked across one of the upstairs bedrooms and vanished. Marlee fled the building!"

According to Maria and Andrew, one psychic shed some light on the woman who appears as a dark shadow. "Upon entering the building, the psychic was overcome by the presence of a distraught woman. As she slowly climbed the stairs to the second floor, four rooms came into view: a child's room, a sewing room, another child's room, and then, the one she felt the most drawn, to the adults' bedroom. A crib stood to one side and mourning clothes were laid upon the bed."

Was her spirit still looking for her child more than a century later? Who designed the room and chose to lay a mourning dress on the bed and to place a crib in the room; and did they know something?

Energy is felt around the crib.

The psychic said, "The details were clear. It was a woman between twenty and twenty-eight. Her pain was overwhelming to me and I felt the need to reach out to the grieving mother. To everyone else present there was nobody in the bedroom, but I knew differently."

A lovely old grandfather clock graces the interior of Burwick House. This is no ordinary clock — it is enchanted. Although the grandfather clock no longer works, it has a tendency to chime when visitors arrive on the second floor and stops when they vacate the premises.

"When the mother and daughter first began to climb the stairs, the pair felt nothing out of the ordinary. Soon after they had reached the second floor, they began to feel cold and unwelcome. The young girl in particular was ill at ease. She felt a soft hand gingerly touch her face and momentarily cup her chin. And then the clock began to chime. It wasn't the peaceful ringing that is so endearing about grandfather clocks. Instead, it sounded ominous somehow, almost agitated. The mother took her child's hand and fled downstairs. Once there, the clock stopped chiming."

In 2003, Jennifer Fulton, an employee at Black Creek Pioneer Village, had a paranormal experience.

"I was working in the Burwick House. On this particular day I was alone in the parlour. There were workmen working outside on the building. I started to walk through the hallway to the kitchen when I suddenly heard men talking downstairs in the basement. I couldn't make out what they were saying. I did know that the staff room was located in the basement. I just thought they were employees taking a break.

"I was still in the kitchen when I saw the livestock girls go downstairs. I told them there were people down in the basement but according to them that was impossible. The staff room was locked up. We went downstairs together and indeed the room was locked and [there was] no sign of anyone. I know I had distinctly heard men's voices in the basement."

One former employee said she felt a very protective energy in the kitchen and up the back stairs. She felt it was a male presence.

In July of 2006, a visitor sensed sadness that seemed to linger in the house. Toronto Ghosts and Hauntings Research Society provided the story.

"Last summer my husband and I took our children to Black Creek Pioneer Village. Upon entering the Burwick House I immediately felt a little uneasy. We passed through the bottom floor of the house and proceeded upstairs. Halfway up the stairs I sensed a horrible feeling of utter sadness and something very sinister.

"At the top of the stairs I felt very uneasy again and wanted to leave. I felt the hair on the back of my neck stand up. I said, 'Let's go' to my husband. He said, 'Wait, I want to see the rooms.' I told him I had seen enough. He simply said, 'Come on' and took my hand.

"We looked in the rooms and I continually had this horrible, strong sense of uneasiness. I turned and told my husband I would meet him outside. My husband of course didn't sense anything."

Apparently this visitor also commented that she felt the sadness or sinister feelings around the cradle in the adults' bedroom on the second floor.

In 2007, on the ghost walk tour of the village, a group shared some experiences with Catherine.

"During this tour we had a number of visitors report strange sensations, feelings, sounds, and sights, while exploring Burwick House. One little girl broke down into hysterics because she felt someone touching the back of her shoulder while she was by an upstairs bedroom door. Another kid felt the icy grip of a cold hand through her thick woollen mitten. One couple reported hearing a crying sound coming from the bedroom. They said it sounded like a sad, mournful wail."

Other people have seen a female spirit who looks out of the second-storey windows. Visitors have felt an entity brush against them as they climb the stairs to the second floor. Catherine herself has sensed the strong feelings of unease. She even broke out into a cold sweat on two occasions.

"I had to pause a few times in the middle of the ghost story to catch my breath and calm myself down. I could literally feel a woman's overpowering presence behind me while I was giving my talk. Several visitors were showing me strange orbs [circles of light] they had caught on their digital cameras. I even captured a few on my camera."

There is an item in the Burwick House that has the power to move on its own — the rocking horse.

The rocking horse is situated in the upstairs bedroom on the right. One employee has just stood there and watched the toy horse rock back and forth, seemingly under its own power. (Could a child be sitting on the horse and rocking it?)

The rocking horse rocks on its own.

The alarm system in the Burwick House is composed of motion sensor units that seem to have the ability to detect spirits moving about at night — an experience had by employees there.

Ruthan Johnson encountered paranormal activity while employed at Burwick. She is quick to point out that the spirit of a woman has been seen at the fireplace on the main floor. She also confirms the presence of a female spirit upstairs where the rocking horse resides.

Ruthan has a story, about Adele, an elderly employee and a direct descendant of the family who once owned the home. She asked her for help with the second-storey window curtains.

"Adele would close the curtains on the three windows facing the street. She would then go downstairs, lock up, and leave the building. Once she was outside she would look up at the second-storey windows and the curtains would be pulled back.

"To help her, I entered the building and went upstairs. I waved to Adele on the street and closed the curtains. I went downstairs and exited the building. I saw Adele and looked up at the windows and the curtains were pulled back again!"

A shadow appears in the doorway of the kitchen.

Ruthan pointed out the butler's pantry; a small room by the office is closed-off from the public by a chain hanging across the middle of the doorway. On occasion, people — Ruthan's husband, Dennis, is one such person — has witnessed this chain swinging back and forth on its own.

Another area of activity in the house is the office downstairs. Ruthan stated, "The office feels like an ice box even in the summer."

Jeff Farrell, a staff interpreter who has worked at Black Creek Pioneer Village for several years, feels the spirit associated with the office is that of a man. Jeff told me he has a female friend, Rhona Hasting, who is a "sensitive." She visited Jeff one time when he was working at Burwick House. According to her, five or six spirits inhabit the house.

Rhona Hasting stated, "In the upstairs of the Burwick House, I would stand there for a very long time as a child. I would look into the rooms and feel at ease, very content. As an adult, I would feel a difference in the atmosphere, more of a sadness. A couple of years ago, I went to the house and had my camera with me. I went upstairs. The camera was hanging around my neck on a strap. Then the camera went crazy and started clicking and winding itself in some way. I was by myself and did feel like I was being told to leave, so I did — very quickly."

There is no question that Burwick House is a busy place, layered in time, beyond the rational mind. Why not visit for yourself and see what experience may await you. Perhaps you may see through the veil of time and embrace the past too.

The Flynn House

~ Black Creek Pioneer Village ~

OCCASIONALLY ATTACHMENT CAN BECOME A PRISON SENTENCE THAT goes beyond the act of death. In some cases, the very prison cell may be the former home and grounds of the deceased. This would seem to be a possible explanation for Mrs. Flynn.

The Flynn House, situated around the corner from the Burwick house, is a small, yellow wooden home, built in 1858. The house originally stood at Yonge Street and Drury Road, just north of Toronto. It was moved to Black Creek Pioneer Village in 1959.

The first occupants of this home were Irish immigrants — Daniel Flynn, his wife, and their two daughters. Daniel was a shoemaker by trade. The rear parlour of the house was used as the boot and shoe shop. Eventually Daniel constructed a shop on the grounds. In 1963, architect Napier Simpson described the building. "This small building has traces of Classical architecture in its facade. No doubt the man who built it was aware of style in architecture. Realizing that his establishment was on a main thoroughfare and would be seen by many hundreds of people a day, he planned a well-designed building.

The size of the building however, presupposes that it could only serve a very small business."

Daniel's original shop in the house later became the kitchen. Two bedrooms were located off the main sitting room area and there was an attic upstairs.

Ruthan Johnson worked in the Flynn House for several years. She loved working in the building and never felt alone because, as it turns out, Mrs. Flynn was there to keep her company.

Ruthan said, "At times Mrs. Flynn would become very playful. I could sense her around. She has been seen wearing a yellow dress. There is a cookstove in the kitchen and a fireplace in the parlour. The staff and I would bake everyday on the cookstove. I would light the fire in the cookstove and wait till I had a nice blaze going. Then I would leave to light a fire in the fireplace.

"One day the fire was going so well in the cookstove that I could actually hear the steam coming out of the kettle but when I returned to the kitchen the fire in the cookstove had gone out. The stove surface was stone cold as if I had never lit a fire."

In addition to these antics, apparently Mrs. Flynn also enjoyed Ruthan's baking.

Daniel Flynn House, 1858

"Every day I would bake cookies and cakes. Once they were out of the oven, I would place the cookies and cakes on a plate and set them down on a nearby table. I would then go to the parlour or to the woodshed for more wood, but upon returning to the kitchen there would be a cookie or cake sitting next to the plate."

Despite the gentle tricks played on Ruthan, not all of Mrs. Flynn's attentions are so benevolent. Catherine Crow explained that there was a story that Mrs. Flynn's husband was abusive to her, which could explain her apparent dislike for men.

Ruthan elaborates: "There was a gentleman who delivered firewood to the houses in Black Creek Pioneer Village. He would often come to the back door of the Flynn House for a freshly baked piece of cake. Mrs. Flynn did not like him. She would bolt the door and close the open window."

One day Ruthan's husband, Dennis, was delivering the firewood.

"As I was walking up the boardwalk to the Flynn House I would hear the bolt slide closed on the back door denying me entry to the home.

"I went around the building, to the front door to give Ruthan heck for locking the back door. I soon discovered that Ruthan had not been anywhere near the back section of the house. Ruthan then asked Mrs. Flynn, out loud, to let me in the back door."

Dennis returned to the back door and heard the bolt slide to allow him entry. This all happened before Ruthan could even get there.

Ruthan understood that Mrs. Flynn still sleeps in one of the bedrooms of the house.

"There are two bedrooms situated directly across from the parlour. When I arrived in the morning I would notice the bed in the bedroom to the right of the parlour had been slept in. There would be an impression of a body having laid in the bed. It was quite visible."

A newly-hired security guard named Mark was working his first night shift when he encountered Mrs. Flynn.

"Mark found himself checking around the Flynn property at 4:00 a.m. when he spotted a woman in a long, yellow, period dress in the garden at the back of the house.

"He cautiously approached the woman with a flashlight in hand and said to her, 'Excuse me, ma'am, but you are not allowed to be on the property.' Just as he reached her, she completely disappeared in front of him."

The experience frightened him so badly that he quit the next day.

Mrs. Flynn has also been seen walking the streets of Black Creek Pioneer Village at night. During the summer, re-enactors often camp out at Black Creek Village. One night, a group that was camping there were socializing on the porch of the Half Way House Inn. The inn is located just up from the Flynn home. Right in front of them a woman in a yellow period dress was seen walking up the street from the Flynn House and she vanished just as she reached the inn. One re-enacter said, "It was almost as if she was floating above the road."

Mrs. Flynn has also been seen on a number of occasions near the rhubarb patch located in the backyard garden. Mrs. Flynn likes to make her presence felt. Ruthan would often smell lavender wafting through the parlour.

Typical of Irish Roman Catholics, the Flynn family had pictures of saints in the house. The picture of one saint is still situated on a wall in the parlour. Two framed pictures of saints hang in the front hall, and one on the fireplace wall and another on the wall between the two bedrooms. Dennis felt that someone liked to change the location of the saints since Saint Patrick had been moved to a new location!

Someone also walks in the attic. Catherine told me the story of an employee named Randy, who had a startling encounter with a spirit in the Flynn House.

"Randy heard distinct footsteps walking upstairs in the attic. The attic is closed to the public. No one ever goes up there. It is an empty room with a small window at the far side that lets in a tiny amount of light."

Randy decided to investigate. Up he went to the attic. No one was there! Down he went to the kitchen.

"Five minutes later he heard the same footsteps above him. There was no doubt in his mind that these were human footsteps.

"Again he went up to the attic. No one was there. Disturbed and leery, he made a hasty retreat to the kitchen. As soon as he sat down in the chair, the footsteps returned. This time the footsteps were louder and angry ... booming from the attic."

Mad at a man? Maybe it's Mrs. Flynn, again!

There is usually activity on the eve of Halloween. A tour guide named

Jeff, who is well aware of Mrs. Flynn's antipathy to men, helped Catherine light the candles in the Flynn House on Halloween.

"Jeff lit one candle and I lit another. I took the first tour group through the house and found it odd that the candle Jeff had lit was already out, almost as if someone had blown it out, while the candle I lit stayed flickering all night. That night Jeff took three groups of visitors into the house. On all three tours people heard distinct footsteps walking above them, in the attic. I had just finished my ghost walk in the Burwick house and was heading to the staff room when John came running out onto the street and told me to come quickly to the Flynn house.

"'Listen!' he instructed. All the visitors in Jeff's group were staring up at the ceiling. Then I heard it. There were distinct shuffling footsteps coming close to the attic stairs."

A ghost with good timing!

The Flynn House has been closed for repairs. This probably makes Mrs. Flynn's day. No more men around for a while. But if you see that yellow dress, do say hello!

The Half Way House Inn

~ Black Creek Pioneer Village ~

JEALOUSY, DECEPTION AND BETRAYAL ARE A RECIPE FOR MISERY, IN THIS lifetime and beyond unless we learn to let go!

Poor Mary Ann Thompson; the wife of innkeeper, Alexander, may have discovered his secret before he died in 1873 — Alexander had another wife.

Mary Ann, it seems, is angry still, walking the hallways and the rooms of the Half Way House Inn at Black Creek Pioneer Village.

She is known as the woman in the blue dress.

The Half Way House Inn was built in 1849 by Alexander Thompson on the well-travelled Kingston Road, on the corner of Midland Avenue and Kingston Road in the Township of Scarborough. The inn was a favourite destination for those taking the stagecoach to Toronto. It was also a focal point for the community, which would use the inn for celebrations, and political and religious meetings.

Catherine Crow described the inn. "The main section of the first floor is the same as it was originally. Upstairs, the five bedrooms on the one side of the hall are also original to the building. The other side of

The Half Way House Inn, 1849

the hallway was divided into a meeting room at the front of the inn and the innkeeper's quarters at the back of the stairs."

Alex Thompson and his wife Mary Ann lived in the inn until his death in 1873. The next owner, Ignatius Galloway, added a dining room and a new kitchen to the first floor. He remodelled the innkeeper's quarters and meeting rooms into a ballroom on the second floor.

The establishment remained an inn until it closed in 1955. The Toronto and Region Conservation Authority acquired the building soon after and moved it to Black Creek Pioneer Village in 1965.

Several years ago, Catherine had the opportunity to speak with Linda, the manager of the restaurant at the inn. She knew a great deal about the woman in the blue dress. "Oh yes, I've seen her and I've heard her too!

"She will tell you the woman in the blue dress spends a lot of time in the ballroom. She has also been spotted looking out over the balcony at the end of the second floor."

The restaurant is another of her favourite haunts. She likes to knock on walls and play with the radio.

"There have been many times when I've locked up at night and turned off the radio in the restaurant, only to open up first thing in the morning to find the radio on playing music. There is no one who comes down here at night so I can't explain why it is turned on.

"There is one location in the restaurant where the spirit knocks. It is in the wall above a table and two chairs situated by the fireplace. This is where you will hear the distinct knocks in the wall."

Luke, another employee at the inn who works as a costume interpreter, has also seen the woman in the blue dress.

Catherine explained, "Luke came into work very early one morning and as he entered the front door of the inn he saw a woman in a blue period dress with long brown hair walking slowly and silently up the staircase to the second floor. Luke assumed it was Alice, who worked at the inn.

"Luke was surprised to see Alice there so early. He said good morning, but received no reply. Luke walked back to the kitchen. Sue, a kitchen staff worker, told Luke that it was Alice's day off!

"Luke went upstairs to look for the woman in the blue dress, curious to discover who she was. He checked every room thoroughly and found absolutely no one."

Ruthan Johnson also encountered some unexplained activity in this building. She could never keep a door shut on the wardrobe in the hallway. She would close the door and come back later to discover it open.

A volunteer named Jacquie also shared a story.

"Whenever the woman in the blue dress is spotted walking up the staircase, she either disappears at the top of the landing or is seen entering the ballroom at the top of the stairs and then disappears. The only trace of her left behind is a subtle scent of perfume."

Has Mary Ann stayed behind because she's angry or still seeking fun in the ballroom — or is she refusing to go to some place where she may have to face Alexander?

Hopefully, one day Mary Ann Thompson can see her way to forgive and move on. Until then she remains lonely, unloved, and imprisoned in the fourth dimension.

The Blacksmith Shop
~ Black Creek Pioneer Village ~

RUTHAN IS A WOMAN FULL OF LIFE WITH AN ACUTE AWARENESS OF HER surroundings. Her husband, Dennis, exudes friendliness and has a natural aptitude for his historical surroundings and responsibilities.

Both Ruthan and Dennis feel like old spirits who have the unique ability to move easily back in time. The couple were formally employed for many years at Black Creek Pioneer Village. Ruthan worked as an historical interpreter, seamstress, and tinsmith during her many years at the village. Dennis was the village blacksmith.

The Rose Blacksmith Shop at the village was originally located in Nobleton, Ontario. The structure dates back to circa 1855. The blacksmith created a wide range of forged iron ware, including hinges, hasps, and tools for use on the farm and in the home. Early blacksmiths also shod horses and oxen and forged iron wheels for wagons.

One unique item that Dennis made was called the courting candle. It was designed to demonstrate the attitude and acceptance of a father to his daughter's suitor.

Dennis explained, "The candle holder had a wooden base attached to an iron spiral form that housed the candle. Using the spiral you could adjust the candle to burn for a determined length of time."

"During the courting ritual, when a suitor visited the home of his lady friend, they would retire to the parlour. The father would adjust the length of the candle to burn according to his observations of the suitor. He would then light the candle and leave. When the candle burned down to the setting the suitor would leave the premises."

Upon returning, the suitor could observe where the candle was set to determine the likelihood of continuing to woo his lady friend. If the candle had been set at a shorter length this meant the father did not approve of this suitor. If the candle setting was increased in length the suitor was closer to seeing more of the lady and eventually they might marry.

Although Dennis had never had any paranormal experiences in the blacksmith shop he has worked in every historical building in the village and had some very personal experiences. This is not to say that nothing of the unexplained has ever occurred in the blacksmith shop. Catherine explained what happened one evening.

"At night, when the lights are turned off, some employees tell me you can faintly hear the sound of horses coming from inside the shop. There is the jingle-jangle sound of metal harnesses, the clomping of hooves clad in horseshoes, as well as soft neighing and snorting sounds."

During the Halloween ghost tour in 2007, Catherine Crow and her group experienced firsthand the sound of horses.

"The doors of the blacksmith shop were open and there were two candle lanterns burning so everyone could see all of the equipment, tables, tools and everything else inside the building. It was a dark night with no breeze. I had just started to talk about horses haunting the building when a distinct sound of jangling metal started up on the right side of the shop, followed by a faint whinny sound. Everyone heard it!!!

"At one time, a worker in the village swore he briefly heard the distinct sound of panicked horses in the shop. He explained, 'It was as if they were trying to flee from some great danger.' In this case, the danger of the fire seems the most likely explanation."

When the blacksmith shop comes to life at night, I, myself, have to wonder if we've just crossed into another time zone — one that is happening simultaneously with our own. Or, is that too much of a quantum leap to consider?

The Dominion Carriage Works and Cabinet Maker's Shop

~ Black Creek Pioneer Village ~

If a candle lighted as part of a ceremony goes out,
it is a sign that evil spirits are nearby

AN UNDERTAKER MAY NEED TO BE CAREFUL TO DIFFERENTIATE BETWEEN the worlds of the living and the worlds of the dead. Working with the dead for a long time may cause confusion about one's own demise. Such may be the case at Black Creek Pioneer Village.

Catherine tells us the cabinet maker was often the local undertaker who also made the coffins. This might explain the spirit in the long, dark topcoat.

The cabinet maker's shop at Black Creek was once the showroom of the Dominion Carriage Works, built in 1860 in Sebringville, Ontario. It was relocated to the pioneer village in 1979.

The Dominion Carriage Works is equipped with twin forges, a carpenter's shop, a trim shop and paint and varnish rooms. The operation of the Carriage Works was a thriving business where wagons, carriages, and sleighs were built and repaired.

The Dominion Carriage Works, 1860

Although Dennis Johnson worked in the blacksmith shop next door, he would on occasion visit the cabinet maker's shop to create the wooden base needed for his courting candles. It was here that he encountered a spirit in the basement of the building.

Dennis explained, "I would go down to the basement of the building where the woodworking shop was housed. There I would create the bases for the courting candles. While I was down there I would often sense someone watching me. I felt that someone was leaning right over my shoulder. It was like 'it' was playing a game. I would relax and then quietly turn around and see a shadow or a movement of someone behind me. You could, on occasion, hear the spirit walking around the space.

"You could also hear 'it' walk to another room. I felt like 'it' was right in my back pocket. It also hangs out around the stairs. I was very uncomfortable."

Dennis commented that spirit in the basement had been very active just prior to the incident.

I took the challenge myself and headed down there. I could feel the menacing discomfort. Touring the basement area alone left me with the same uncomfortable feeling that Dennis had talked about. I could not wait to climb back up the stairs to safety.

What Dennis had encountered has become known as "the ghost in the long, dark coat."

Ray is an older employee of Black Creek Pioneer Village and worked in the cabinet maker's shop for many years. Catherine described him as a down-to-earth gentleman who is very matter of fact when talking about the spirit who haunts this building.

"Ray described the ghost as a middle-aged man who wears a long, dark topcoat and a brimmed hat. Ray has never been able to see his face. He [the ghost] walks through a closed door at the back of the room and visits for up to four or five minutes before he slowly disappears.

"The spirit also liked to hang around the back of the cabinet maker's shop to look over Ray's shoulder while he was busy doing woodworking."

(Perhaps he was inspecting Ray's work!)

"Ray told us that when the ghost is not busy visiting the shop, he resides upstairs above the shop. Employees and visitors alike can hear his footsteps from time to time."

The room upstairs is only used as a storage space.

Chris, another employee, encountered the spirit in the long dark coat when he first started working in the cabinet maker's shop. One day he was asked to take a bucket downstairs and fill it with water. Here's what happened.

Cabinet maker's shop basement where people see the phantom undertaker.

"As he was busy filling the bucket he saw out of the corner of his eye, a man in a long, dark coat walk behind him and then disappear into a small room at the back of the basement."

Chris thought it was James, another employee, but when he said hello, there was no reply. He thought that was odd. Sometime later in the day, Chris went downstairs again for water. The same man in a long, dark coat walked behind him and disappeared into the back room of the basement.

Chris said hello again, and once more there was no reply. He decided to confront James about that but when he walked into the back room there was no one there. Chris was alone. This had to be Ron's ghost. Soon after the incident, Chris transferred to a building in the village not known for a resident ghost.

Catherine Crow decided to visit the cabinet maker's shop with her camera.

"I was drawn to the coffin standing at the back of the room by the door where the ghost often makes his entrance. The first photograph I took was covered in orbs all around the doorway and the coffin itself. The second time I went to take a picture my flashbulb literally exploded with light and the entire photograph was covered with a white hazy mist. The bottom outline of the coffin was the only thing that could be seen in the photograph."

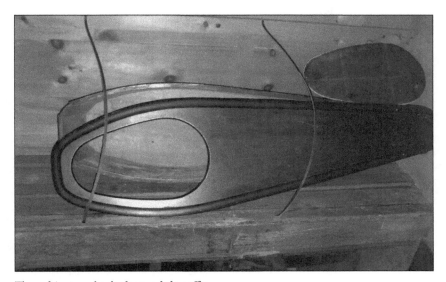

The cabinet maker's shop, adult coffin.

Catherine and another employee, named Karrell, decided that the time had come to explore the space upstairs; the space where "the spirit" lives.

This is what happened.

"Karrell and I mounted the only staircase that led to the second floor. We made our way ... to a door that opened up into the room above the shop. As soon as Karrell and I walked into the darkened room, we were overcome with identical sensations of unease and with a feeling of heavy pressure on our chests, and a tingling chill sensation down both arms.

"Karrell would go no further into the room. I slowly made my way down to the back of the room; the strange pressure and tingling sensation became stronger with each step I took. At the back of the room there was an old wooden bench and I felt certain this ghostly man was sitting on it and watching both of us with a certain amount of interest and curiosity."

The spirit activity continues here. On one ghost tour, as the group approached the cabinet maker's shop, it appeared as though they were expected.

"As soon as we approached the porch, the front door mysteriously opened wide for us. There was no one behind the door and it was a still night.

"The members of the group were astonished to witness an invitation to enter. In fact, many of the visitors laughed nervously. They weren't laughing as they left the building!

"As the last visitor stepped through the door it closed mysteriously and firmly, much to everyone's surprise and shock."

Be careful touring the Carriage Works ... the undertaker may very well be measuring you up before you leave!

OTHER ONTARIO HAUNTS

The Elgin and
Winter Garden Theatre
~ Toronto, Ontario ~

Professional actors consider it a bad sign if a rehearsal is perfect.
The play will have a very short run after a perfect rehearsal, or will
go very badly. Similarly, it is extremely unlucky to speak the tag
line, or the last line of the play, during rehearsals.

MARCUS LOEWS FELT THAT THE ARCHITECTURE AND DECORATION OF HIS theatres was meant to be just as entertaining as what was being presented on stage. Little did Marcus know that in 1982, the two theatres together would be declared a National Historic site. The last, stacked (one theatre on top of another), Edwardian theatre in the world.

The site is also one of the most enchanting haunted locations in all of Canada. These two theatres were originally built by Marcus Loews as a flagship. His motto was, "We sell tickets to theatres not shows." Marcus was born on May 7, 1887, in Queens, New York, into a poor, Jewish family. He left school at the age of nine to sell newspapers and lemons on the street. Marcus continued to work hard and started and failed at more than one business venture. He was bankrupt before he reached the age of twenty.

Then Marcus met Adolph Zukor, who became his friend and partner. Marcus purchased Zukor's penny arcade business and set about expanding it across the United States.

During an opening of an arcade in Cincinnati, he was told of a competitor who was successful with motion pictures rather than mechanical machines. He promptly struck a deal with the Vitagraph Company for the necessary equipment and films, borrowed chairs, and based on nickel admissions, grossed almost $250 that very first day!

In New York, he bought a Brooklyn burlesque house and converted it into the Royal, a first class house that mixed vaudeville bills and movies.

Next, Marcus made a deal with brothers Joseph and Nicholas Schenck to form the Fort George Amusement Company in 1906. Over the next decade he worked on a slow and methodical plan to obtain theatrical dominance. By November of 1918, he owned 112 theatres throughout North America that offered the mix of vaudeville and movies.

He died on September 5, 1927 at the age of fifty-seven, bequeathing a $30-million-dollar estate to his wife, Caroline, and his sons. According to the Ontario Heritage Trust, "This complex was the Canadian flagship of Marcus Loew's legendary theatre chain and was designed by Thomas Lamb, as a double-decker theatre complex. It contained the Winter Garden Theatre, which was constructed seven storeys above Loew's Yonge Street Theatre (renamed the Elgin Theatre in 1978)."

The Davies Takacs Lobby has been the scene of several paranormal encounters.

The Winter Garden Theatre

Loew's Yonge Street Theatre opened on December 15, 1913, and on February 16, 1914, the Winter Garden Theatre opened. The Ontario Heritage Trust adds, "The two theatres were distinct; the Elgin was all gold leaf and rich fabrics, a formal theatre of plaster cherubs and ornate opera boxes. The Winter Garden Theatre was a botanical fantasy, its walls hand-painted to resemble a garden, its ceiling a mass of real beech boughs and twinkling lanterns."

The gold-and-marble domed "hard top" lower theatre (The Elgin) was home to continuous vaudeville shows and movies. The upper level, the Winter Garden Theatre, was an atmospheric country garden beneath the stars. This theatre was built for the big-time vaudeville market, and it had reserved seats at premium prices, that catered to the middle class. As well as competing in a different market, the upper theatre was used for theatrical experimentation without posing the risk of closing the lower theatre.

~ ~ ~

The Ontario Heritage Trust describes the acts, "The theatres played host to such great acts as George Burns and Gracie Allen, Sophie Tucker, Milton Berle, and Edgar Bergen and Charlie McCarthy."

According to the Elgin and Winter Garden Theatre booklet, "Loew's Yonge Street Theatre was the larger of the two theatres, seating 2,149. The Winter Garden Theatre seated 1,410 patrons.

"The Elgin could accommodate a show that consisted of eight to ten vaudeville acts, interspersed with newsreels and a silent movie. This downstairs theatre was the 'grind' house, with continuous daily shows starting at 11:00 a.m. The Winter Garden Theatre was intended as the more prestigious of the two theatres, featuring higher ticket prices, reserved seating, and a single evening performance."

The popularity of vaudeville declined with the advent of talking pictures. In May of 1928, the Winter Garden Theatre was closed. The theatre remained closed for more than half a century, a time capsule of a bygone era. Loew's Yonge Street Theatre (The Elgin) remained open.

By the 1960s, the staircase leading up to the Winter Garden Theatre was hidden behind a partition wall and a drop ceiling. The existence of the Winter Garden Theatre was all but forgotten.

The Elgin Theatre continued to operate as a movie house. As the decades passed the theatre gradually slipped into disrepair. On March 17, 1978, Leow's Yonge Street Theatre was renamed The Elgin Theatre.

In 1981, the Ontario Heritage Trust purchased the building. Prior to launching into a massive restoration of the theatres, the successful production of *Cats* ran for nearly two years at the Elgin Theatre. The Trust adds, "The most successful pre-sales theatrical event in Canada at the time."

In 1987, a $29 million restoration initiative of the building and the two theatres was begun. The trust describes this awesome task of restoration and the treasures that were found during the process.

"The gilt plaster detail work in the Elgin Theatre required more than three-hundred thousand wafer-thin sheets of aluminium leaf. The walls of the Winter Garden Theatre had to be cleaned using fifteen-hundred pounds of raw dough to avoid damaging the original hand-painted watercolour artwork."

According to the Elgin and Winter Garden booklet, "The Winter Garden Theatre's most unusual aspect, its leafy ceiling, was still intact; the leaves, brittle and dust-covered, had to be replaced. For this purpose more than five thousand real beech branches were harvested, preserved, painted, fireproofed, and woven into wire grids suspended from the theatre ceiling.

"In the downstairs Elgin Theatre, major plaster elements [including the theatre opera boxes] had been removed and the original colour scheme obscured by as many as twenty-seven layers of paint in some areas. Using the original design drawings and historic photographs as guides, missing elements were faithfully recreated, damaged elements repaired, and the original colour scheme accurately restored."

The Trust states, "More than sixty-five thousand square feet of new space was created, including the lobby and lounge areas, and an eight-storey backstage pavilion housing modern dressing rooms and two rehearsal halls."

On December 15, 1989, the Elgin and Winter Garden Theatres re-opened. "The theatres have once again become one of finest theatrical stage complexes.

"One of the greatest treasures discovered during the restoration, is the world's largest collection of vaudeville scenery — hand-painted flats and drops dating from 1913. Several restored pieces, including the magnificent Butterfly and Scarab Scenery Flats, are now displayed in the theatre centre."

Imagine an entire theatre, intact with all its decor, sealed up for so many years! A perfect recipe for spirit activity, time travel, and spiralling energy! Is this the case?

According to Cecilia Aguilera, an employee who works in the box office located in the lobby of the theatre, "We are not haunted, nor are we petrified. The theatre is like a vortex of energy."

Late one afternoon this past fall (2013) I met Linda Atkinson, who had agreed to tour me through the building. Linda is a delightful and informative volunteer tour guide of the theatres. She displays enthusiasm and shares a deep connection to the historical perspective of the Elgin and Winter Garden Theatres and to the spirits who come and go in the building. She is very aware of, and familiar with, the spirits and the energy that inhabit the structure. She described many of the areas of the building where one can potentially see a spirit and experience spiralling energy.

She began with the spirit they call the Lilac or Lavender Lady. During the 2002 theatre season there were four months when the Winter Garden Theatre was "black" (a term used to describe a time when no shows are playing). There is a superstition that an emptied theatre, left completely dark, will invite a ghost to take up residence. Another version of the same superstition claims that the ghosts of past performances return to the stage to relive their glory moments. To prevent this, a single light is left burning at centre stage after the audience, actors, and musicians have gone.

It was during this black time that Cecilia and a co-worker, who is a medium, went up to the Winter Garden Theatre to check on a seating plan.

Cecilia describes a spirit encounter in the Winter Garden Theatre.

"We went together because we did not want to be up there alone. We opened the doors to the theatre and were greeted by a beautiful lilac smell. It was like walking into a garden. We carried on with our business. I went back later to the theatre doorway, but the smell was gone. It was a girl. I just know it. Some people smell lilac and other visitors smell lavender. We call her the Lilac/Lavender Lady."

Linda described a time when she and Cecilia had an unexplained encounter in the box office in the lobby.

"I was in the doorway of the box office and Cecilia was sitting in a chair inside the office. [For some background, from 1913 to 1919, where the box office is today was once Helen's House of Hats, a retail store in the theatre]. I could feel this swirling energy behind me. It went past me and Cecilia could feel something go by her. The energy never made a sound." Cecilia believes this swirling energy is associated with a spirit. She said, "The spirit gets bored and wants some company!"

This spring Cecilia and two volunteers, Stephen and Tim, heard something.

"I was sitting in the box office and the guys were next door. Tim suddenly heard a whistle. He came around to see if I had heard it. A minute later, Stephen appeared around the corner and said, 'who whistled?' There was no one else present at the time."

Whistling is expressly prohibited in the theatre, pertaining to all parts of the building, particularly the dressing rooms, where it is said that if heard, someone (not necessarily the whistler) will soon be out of work. The reason for this superstition is that prior to the advent of walkie-talkies, cues for theatre technicians were called with a sailor's whistle. Therefore, one who whistles in a theatre may, inadvertently, call a cue before its time, and set all manner of catastrophes into action. Should this happen, someone would likely get fired.

One theatre usher wrote in to the Toronto and Ontario Ghosts and Hauntings Research Society and referred to the Lilac/Lavender Lady with this story: "There is a female patron who is believed to have been stabbed in the Winter Garden Theatre washroom [that is now closed]. She dragged herself to the elevator [the elevator is operated by ushers] where she waited, but no one came. She died there. ... A lot of ushers, including myself, [without touching the controls] have been taken up to the fifth floor [Winter Garden Theatre level], but there is no one there. Sometimes there are not even any shows playing there at the time."

Linda's story is a little different. She related a story involving a "sensitive" named Marian, who visited in 2011, during the Doors Open Ontario event.

"Marian had seen an ad in the paper advertising the Doors Open event at the theatre. She had never been nor had any knowledge of the place prior, but knew she needed to visit the Winter Garden Theatre and unexpectedly ended up in the fourth row in both theatres despite hundreds of people in the room.

"She told me she could see a scene unfolding, very much like watching a movie. This is what she had to say. "The Lilac Lady is in the balcony. She secretly followed her husband to work. She suspected her husband of having an affair.

"He arrived at the box office with a lady friend and purchased two tickets. His wife, who was following some distance behind, purchased a ticket for an opera box seat in order to observe him. Once everyone had been seated she stood up and glared down at her husband in the audience seats. This caused quite a commotion. He called out to her. He knew she could ruin him if she wanted to do so.

"The wife fled up the balcony stairs. The husband pursued her. He caught her in the women's washroom. He beat her about the face until she bled. The husband then fled the theatre with his female companion.

"The wife was bloody from the violent encounter. The wife then crawled to the elevator but she did not die as a result of the beating.'"

Linda and Marian then walked up the stairs to the balcony box where the woman had been seated.

The chair in the box office where the Lilac/Lavender Lady sits.

Linda continued, "As soon as we entered the box, Marian turned her attention to the third chair. I sat down in the chair. I no sooner sat down than I felt absolutely frigid. I had to get out of that seat. Marian said, 'It is the Lilac Lady.' While we were standing in the opera box we were engulfed in a scent of lilac. It lasted for only half a minute."

Linda adds, "Production people often see a lady in this box. When someone goes up to the balcony box to tell her that she must leave the theatre, they find that she has vanished."

I contacted Marian and asked her to share her experience in the Winter Garden Theatre. "When I entered this theatre I had asked Linda if this theatre was haunted. When I walked up the aisle to the back of the theatre I felt a chill. I felt something had passed through me. I could feel a cold spot there.

"I was drawn to an opera box on the right side of the theatre. Linda took me upstairs to the balcony. There were four seats in the area. I could smell cheap lilac water.

"I kept standing up and looking down to the seat where I was seated in both the Elgin Theatre and Winter Garden Theatre and realized I was put there for a reason. I wanted to point my finger at a man that occupied the seat I was in earlier."

Marian described the cheating husband. "He had red hair parted on the side. He wore a cardboard collar, tie, and waistcoat. He had a handle-bar mustache. His lady friend wore a white hat with paper flowers going all around the rim.

"I could see him looking up and seeing her/me. He ran up the aisle while the wife took the hallway towards the ladies room on the upper level." Linda, another tour guide and I all felt a cold spot up there as well. I envisioned him running up the steps and following his wife into the washroom. She threatened his career and in turn he beat her viciously. He was livid and brutal. Afterwards he stops to wash the blood off his hands in the vintage basin. I believe this man to be a well-known banker from Bay Street.

"I see her crawling out of the washroom to the elevator."

This was only one of the spirits Marian witnessed that day. She also saw the spirit of a young girl.

"I saw her by the original box office in the front of the theatre building. Her name is Annie. The last initial is E. She is a child street walker. She has curly brown hair. Her appearance is bedraggled. She is unkempt and wearing an old outfit. She often begged for spare change as the patrons came in and out of the theatre doors."

Marian encountered other spirits in the Elgin Theatre. "Inside this theatre I was aware of the number fifteen. What was that? I instinctively went to the front of the theatre and counted back fifteen rows of seats on the left side-mid row. I saw the spirit of a man wearing a brown hat and a tweed suit. Many cast members have also seen this man in a brown suit and warned him this was a closed set, only to see him disappear.

"Then I observed a very burly gentleman with suspenders and a plaid shirt standing at the very top level of the theatre. He had his arms folded. Then he was gone. I got the feeling he was the projectionist."

A year later, Marian returned to meet Linda with her friend Andrea and a camera. They were not to be disappointed. The spirits of the theatre seem pleased enough to make another appearance.

Marian stated, "Standing at the steps just inside the lobby I saw a shadow of a man cross the room where the bar is. I also smelled cigar smoke — cherry tobacco." According to Linda, this area was the retail store and later, an expanded lobby to accommodate patrons coming down from the Winter Garden.

Andrea described the experience this way. "I saw something zoom by at the end of the bar."

Andrea, Marian and Linda then entered the Elgin Theatre. Andrea described what happened.

"The first thing I did was look up at the second balcony box on the left near the stage. I saw a purple flash. It was a woman wearing a light purple dress."

Marian added, "We heard mumblings of people below. Andrea took a picture. To her amazement some of the spirit forms showed up in the photograph!"

According to Andrea, "At one point we sat in the Elgin Theatre and listened quietly for about half an hour. We then asked the question out loud, 'Is there anybody there?' We were shocked when we heard some mumbling."

Marian added, "We definitely heard voices."

The ladies then visited the backstage of the Winter Garden Theatre. In the first dressing room Marian caught sight of another spirit.

"I saw a very young female around fourteen years old. Her hair was in ringlets. She was a hoofer [professional dancer] who worked multiple shows. I could see her with a director and many prominent people over a long period of time. She had to earn a living any way she could."

Marian had a very unusual experience when they visited the second dressing room. "It looked just like it did when the theatre first opened. The young hoofer didn't like sharing this room with others. She felt entitled."

When I asked Andrea what she thought of all these spirits in the theatre building she replied, "I am pretty savvy when it comes to the spirit world. I have a good friend who is a famous American medium living in California. Spirits are around us all the time. We just need to raise our vibration in order to see. Spirits get attached to certain things and buildings."

In 2011, Linda toured a group of young children through the Winter Garden Theatre. "During the tour, a young girl of six and a boy a little older saw a female spirit on the stage. The girl commented that she was wearing a purple dress. The little boy said there was green on the dress."

Linda mentioned another unusual encounter in the Winter Garden Theatre. "One time someone from the theatre staff and a visitor were in the upper balcony looking down at the stage when the first two rows of theatre seats went down and then back up." Possibly the work of invisible patrons?

There are three old-fashioned elevators still in operation in the building. The elevator to the extreme left is the haunted one. That elevator and the one next to it date back to 1913 when the theatre first opened.

Linda stated that during another tour, a woman admitted to being sensitive to the spirit energy in the building. She and Linda both experienced a swirling energy on the staircase just before the third-floor landing. They went all the way to the fifth floor and Linda said, "It was like standing in a crowd of invisible people. One minute they were there and the next minute they were gone."

Perhaps that area, and that elevator, are a portal!

Linda's companion also felt a cold spot in front of the left elevator.

The old elevators are manually operated from inside the elevator. When you step in and press your floor, you just may not arrive where you expect to arrive.

"I have been in this elevator [the middle elevator] and pressed the button for the fourth floor. The elevator proceeded to the second floor. I pressed four again and it went to the fifth floor."

This is where Linda felt the spirit pass through her.

The theatre elevators. The elevator on the extreme left is reported to be haunted.

The Toronto and Ontario Ghosts and Hauntings Research Society reported another spirit in the Winter Garden Theatre. Three theatre staff conducted a session with an Ouija board. "As soon as they started, a ghost named Samuel identified himself. He had been a trombone player in 1918, and had passed away after falling into the orchestra pit.

"The volunteers asked if there were any other spirits there. He said 'yes', but when they asked to talk to them, he refused."

Linda acknowledged, "A trombone player named Sam, had, apparently, at some point in time, arrived late for work, drunk. He fell into the orchestra pit, a drop of eight feet, and broke his neck. People have reported hearing the sounds of a trombone or saxophone playing in the theatre when it is empty of patrons."

Linda escorted me through the seats below the balcony and through a curtain to a corridor that leads to the back stage. She had a story about this area. "It was here by the lower curtain that a tour guide saw a figure walk past the opening of the curtain." She also mentioned that in the corridor by the backstage doorway you can sometimes feel the swirling energy.

Linda showed me to an area of energy on the stage. Then we proceeded through another doorway that leads to the historical display area. A metal bar is placed on the floor to keep the door open by the display. Linda had an incredible experience here once, while standing a distance across from the doorway.

"I heard this grating sound and looked to see the metal bar moving on its own towards me. The door was slowly closing."

Linda is not the only person to have had a paranormal experience in this exact area.

"During a tour, a lady who was standing by the door kept raising her hand and swatting the air around her head. A witness to the event actually saw her hair move. This lady felt someone tugging on her hair two times." Linda believes this is a male presence and could be Sam, who has a reputation as being a bit of a trickster.

A former employee had this to say, in a letter to the Toronto and Ontario Ghosts and Hauntings Research Society. "One young lady, I believe to have been an actress, has been seen leaving the second floor coat-check room. It has been stated that this area was once a quick-change for the actors.

"There is also a man who stays in and around the second-floor ladies washroom. He is thought to have been a theatre technician."

Entrance to the back stage where Linda senses some swirling energy.

The entrance to the building is the lobby of the Elgin Theatre. On the left a beautiful staircase leads up to the next floor. Here visitors, and theatre staff, report seeing the apparition of a woman in Edwardian clothing. She has, on occasion, lingered long enough to be seen by a few patrons before vanishing.

Linda added, "I did a tour earlier this year [2013]. At the time there was a sign in the lobby advertising a show. A man in the tour saw a form materialize beside the sign and then disappear. On another tour, an actor from England had just come through the archway in the lobby when he felt two taps on his shoulder."

Linda has something to reveal about the Edwardian Lady herself.

"I usually feel her behind me. You feel a pool of energy in the area of the lobby where the gift shop is located, and by the staircase leading up to the elevators.

Edwardian lady appears standing on the lobby staircase.

"Six years ago I was taking part in a private paranormal tour of the theatre. I could feel someone behind me. I was standing on the lobby landing with my back to the centre railing of the staircase. I asked my friends if they could see anyone behind me. They said no. I went to step away, but could not move. I was literally vibrating. I could not stop. At the same time I felt that the female spirit had passed right through me!"

Over the years visitors and staff have reported seeing a lady in Edwardian clothing on the grand staircase. She is referred to as the Edwardian Lady. Linda believes that it is her energy that she has experienced on several occasions in this area. It is always a warm comforting experience.

During a public tour, two ladies, interested in the paranormal, got the surprise of their lives. One of the women took a picture, exactly where Linda had her experience. To their amazement, the form of a woman appeared on their camera, eight steps up, to their right. Linda commented, "It looked like a moving haze."

The Palladian Lounge is another area where people have a physical experience of a spirit. One employee felt three taps on the shoulder there.

In the Elgin Theatre, one of the managers, while standing onstage, was looking up at the middle balcony (middle section) and saw one seat go down, then back up and then the next seat did the same thing. This was during the production of *Cats*.

Lobby area where the Edwardian Lady is seen.

Linda continued, "The production crews and actors often see a man in an old-fashioned tweed suit to the right side of the stage during rehearsals in the Elgin Theatre. Another male spirit is seen in the upper corner of the Elgin. People have seen him just watching what's going on. He may have been one of the original projectionists."

The Toronto and Ontario Ghosts and Hauntings Research Society reported on their website that a little boy fell to his death from one of the balcony boxes in the Elgin Theatre. Apparently he has been seen in and around the box and running up and down the grand staircase from the balcony to the mezzanine.

During the Halloween tour of 2013 three theatre ushers attended and shared their experiences that happened when they worked in the building. Linda was there and she related to me what they had to say. "One female usher saw a young boy running up and down the stairs. She went to find him but he was not there and none of the other ushers had seen him. She also smelled lavender in the Winter Garden Theatre.

"Another usher, while checking the Winter Garden Theatre's back stairs, heard footsteps right behind her and fled the theatre. The third usher smelled lavender in the Winter Garden Theatre."

Linda spoke with another usher who told her, before the tour, that she had worked at the theatre since 2009 and had never had a paranormal experience. That is, until 2013.

"When I was doing the Halloween 2013 tour in the Winter Garden Theatre this same usher saw the Edwardian or White Lady. She said that she was wearing an all-white dress with a high, lace-neck collar and there were two rows of buttons coming down the front of the dress. She was absolutely delighted to have seen her. I guess some of the theatre residents were on the tour that night."

There is one other unusual tale associated with the Winter Garden Theatre. During the renovations in the 1980s, period theatre seats were needed. The restoration staff discovered that the Biograph Theatre in Chicago had similar seating for sale.

The theatre seats were purchased and transported to Toronto. The Toronto and Ontario Ghosts and Haunting Research Society reported, "When the seats arrived, one chair seemed inexplicably to be upholstered in a different colour. Shortly thereafter, the restoration staff were in touch with the Biograph Theatre and discovered the reason for the difference. The chair had intentionally been its unique colour to indicate that it was the last theatre chair to be occupied by the notorious American gangster, John Dillinger. The infamous bank robber and murderer was gunned down outside the Biograph Theatre on July 22, 1934, at about 10:30 p.m."

Unfortunately, the information came too late. John Dillinger's chair had already been reupholstered to match the other theatre seats. Perhaps without knowing it you could be seated in John Dillinger's former chair! There have been no reports of anyone seeing the spirit of this famous gangster in the Winter Garden Theatre ... yet!

Marcus Loew was quite right about architecture and decoration being as entertaining as the talent performing on stage. What he did not realize was that the creation of these theatres would be so alluring and breathtaking that some people would never leave. In fact, the entire building exists in a time warp or as Cecilia stated "a vortex of energy," that is quite revealing and at other times, mysterious and haunting, certainly, not to be forgotten.

The Cawthra Estate

~ Mississauga, Ontario ~

MUSE WITH ME A WHILE...

Grace Cawthra, a slim, graceful woman, stares out her window. She is contemplating her unsatisfied need to understand the world around her. Attachment to her imposing past leaves her yearning to preserve her majestic estate.

Her old world is rapidly disappearing. The iron gates out front remain closed, denying entry and protecting her from change. She has no heirs to carry on and maintain the British traditions. Strong thoughts and passionate memories dominate her character. Desperate to maintain the Cawthra name, does she decide to remain behind to keep that heritage going with her spirit?

The story of the Cawthra family begins with Joseph, born in 1759 at Yeadon, Yorkshire, England. The Cawthras had been cloth manufacturers and owned fine estates in England.

In 1781 Joseph married Mary Turperry in England. By 1800, the couple had emigrated to New York City to begin a new life. Anti-British sentiment forced the family to flee to York (Toronto) in Upper Canada in 1803.

Joseph, who claimed to be a United Empire Loyalist, received 600 acres of land through Crown Grants issued by the British Crown in what is now the City of Mississauga. He registered for the land grant on July 6, 1804, with the order and patent arriving five years later on November 8, 1809.

Throughout his life Joseph engaged in various business ventures. According to author Alison B. Nobbs in an article about the Cawthra family, Joseph had business interests in Geneva, New York, and took goods such as flour to New York and brought back tea to sell in York. He opened the first apothecary store in York in 1806. It was later expanded into a general store. He also dealt in real estate.

Joseph and Mary raised nine children. His son, William, became a financial genius. He managed the family store in York and concentrated on investments. When he died in 1880 he was worth three million dollars. He died without a will, which meant his money went half to his wife, and the other half was divided amongst his brothers and sisters.

John, another of Joseph's sons, was involved in politics and represented Simcoe County in Upper Canada's Parliament. Outside of politics he was a successful merchant and the father of five children.

His youngest son, Henry Cawthra, became a lawyer. When William Cawthra, the financial wizard, died, Henry received a substantial inheritance which allowed him to quit his law practice and spend more time raising his children. Henry taught his sons and daughters to be proud of their British heritage. His daughter, Grace Millicent Kennaway Cawthra, decided to make sure her British roots were never overlooked.

Her mother was Anna Celista Mills, whose family had resided in Hamilton after fleeing the American Revolution in 1793. Her father, Henry, became a stockbroker, a director of the Band of Toronto for more than thirty years, and a director of both the Consumers' Gas Company and the Canada Permanent Mortgage and Loan Company.

Grace Cawthra was first educated by an English governess and later sent to France to study. Her father was very determined to control the fate of his remaining daughter. Despite her dominating parents, Grace was reputed to be the first girl in Toronto to receive a driver's license.

When her father died in 1909, Grace was twenty-six years of age and still unmarried. Her father did leave her an allowance in his will.

In an article entitled "A History of the Cawthra Elliot Estate," author Ken Phipps wrote about Grace's life at the time. "Grace was never left alone. She was chaperoned everywhere she went. During one trip to England she saw many eligible bachelors despite being heavily supervised. She was courted by a member of the Rolls family and her mother accordingly bought a Rolls Royce and toured Scotland with her daughter."

At the onset of World War I, Grace was almost engaged to a Scotsman named Nicholson, who had looks, position, money, and charm, but, Phipps said, "According to Al Smouter, who was Grace's groundskeeper, she loved this man passionately, but her mother told her that if she married him she would be cut out of the will."

During the war she declined to write to him even when he was reportedly taken prisoner of war. However, when Grace learned that he had died in the German camp where he had been held, she apparently regretted her neglect of him.

Grace was also pursued at this time by another suitor named Colonel Harry McIntyre Elliot. The colonel was the son of a major-general of good Cheltenham English stock and during the war he served as a member of the Militia Council in Ottawa. Harry was welcomed into the Cawthra home, but Grace's mother still kept her from marrying and leaving home by threatening to disown her financially. Harry was a patient suitor.

Anna Cawthra passed away in 1921. Grace then agreed to marry Harry under the condition that he would add the name of Cawthra to his own. He also had to agree to ignore, for the rest of his life, the existence of his son and two daughters, at that point adults, whom he had with his first wife, Blanche A. Wickwire of Halifax.

Phipps wrote of one other highly unusual request, "As well, before Grace consented, Harry ostensibly agreed that they would never consummate their marriage; Grace wanted to remain an unadulterated Cawthra, and this was supposedly why she and her husband had separate beds. Grace herself, later in life, claimed she had had a miscarriage — somehow consummation did occur."

On the day of the wedding Grace panicked and phoned Harry and her sister-in-law Ada, to tell them that they may as well stay at home because that's what she was going to do. They rushed over to soothe and placate her until she assented to go. Supposedly Ada said, "Grace, you can leave him at the church door, but marry him you must, why I have the house full of flowers for the reception." At the ceremony Grace was reported to look cold and somewhat diffident. They were married at St. Alban's Cathedral in Toronto on June 29, 1921. At the time of their marriage Grace was forty-three years of age and Harry was fifty-four.

By 1926, Grace had become passionate and fixated on preserving the Cawthra heritage. This intensified with the construction of a Georgian-style mansion on the property granted to her forefather, Joseph Cawthra in 1804.

Although the Cawthra land was about 50 percent swamp, Grace was not deterred. The land was drained, leaving a small pond, which she called "My Lake." Grace employed the English architect, William Lyon Summerville, to design the house, supposedly similar to Yeadon Hall, the family's ancestral home in Yorkshire, England. The bricks used in the construction of the mansion came from the original Cawthra home in Toronto, Yearn Hall.

Not satisfied with a Canadian-style garden, she hired landscape architect Edwin Kay. He sought to design gardens of conservative elegance that enhanced the natural landscape. His philosophy was that a properly designed estate should have a house and landscape that are both aesthetically pleasing and dependent on one another. Kay created an eclectic garden with such elements as a ten-foot-walled garden, serpentine paths, and manicured grassy areas, which contrasted with the wild and unspoiled forestland.

Grace employed English gardeners to maintain the grounds. It seemed that Grace was creating a setting that could transport her back in time. Then she called her estate Cawthre-Lotten. This title represented the family name and the physical location of the lot in Toronto Township. Thus, the parcel's legal description was part of lot ten, or Lotten.

In order to preserve her heritage, and the illusion of that heritage, she held lavish garden parties and pheasant hunts. On July 16, 1934, she held a garden party to celebrate the 150th anniversary of the founding of the United Empire Loyalists, as well as the 130th anniversary of the order-in-council by George III granting the land on which Cawthra-Lotten stood.

On July 14, 1947, the mansion was struck by lightning. Awakened by a rumbling noise at 2:30 a.m. Grace, thinking it was a vandal, woke Harry who looked out his window to see the reflection of flames.

A neighbour had already called the Fire Brigade. When he realized the main gates were locked, Harry, then eighty years old, ran from the house in his robe to unlock the gates. Taxi drivers and onlookers assisted in carrying out paintings and other valuables from the burning guest wing. The three-foot-thick walls checked the progress of the flames enough that the Brigade managed to put the fire out before it reached the main house. Several personal items, including Grace's mother's heirloom wedding dress, were lost. Poor Harry suffered a case of pneumonia from the cool night air during the fire and never really recovered. He passed away on June 27, 1949.

Shortly after her husband's death Grace began to exhibit bouts of paranoia. She suspected people in the household of petty theft. She even created a large notice and posted it in the glass door of a bookcase that read, 'Thou shalt not steal'.

Grace then stopped buying clothes, instead converted Harry's coats and pants into skirts and tied her wispy hair with bits of ribbon. It seemed Grace was beginning to lose her attention concerning the present. She was slipping into the remote past where mysterious aspirations surfaced.

Longing for intimacy and companionship, it is said that Grace would enter the living room late in the evening. She would light the candles and turn off the lights, once she had placed the Ouija board on the table. Then, taking a seat, she would stretch her arms out until her fingers just touched the rim of the crystal glass positioned in the centre of the board. She would call out to Harry, beckoning him to return to her and help to part the darkness that enveloped her. In secrecy she communicated with the dead.

Concerned about neglecting the exterior presence of the estate, she hired a contractor in 1958 to restore the grounds but afterwards she refused to pay for maintenance and the grounds grew wild once again. By now Grace only left the estate for medical appointments. The outside world no longer presented itself in keeping with her virtues. Her niece Mildred Brock visited the Cawthra Estate in 1964. She later recorded her observations. "Grace lives in a world by herself, peopled only by the past."

The stately residence was, for the most part, intact, but was beginning to show signs of wear. Grace herself was preventing the care of the home because she was remaining attached to the past. The dining-room table was permanently set for eight without plates or placemats, in accordance with military custom. Could this have been an act of remembrance of her late husband? Perhaps Harry joined her, in some ghostly fashion, for a meal or two.

"The tables, chairs, and sideboard were piled with unpaid bills, magazines, letters, photos, and boxes of old medicine bottles, and over it all was fifteen years of dust and grime. The living room was littered with china, cushions, and old coats," stated Phipps.

Grace fought change most of her life. Her faithful English housekeeper, Elizabeth Naismith, followed her directions that nothing be touched. Elizabeth was available twenty-four hours a day, seven days a week, except for Wednesday afternoons, when she would unfailingly take the streetcar to Greenwood to wager between two and four dollars on the horse races.

In 1966, Al Smouter and his family moved into the gate-house of the Cawthra Estate. Al was a policeman who decided to take on the part-time job as groundskeeper for Grace. By then, Elizabeth, the housekeeper, was a mere fixture of the estate. For the past ten years she had been taking angina pills for a heart condition. She continued to live in the attic despite the long narrow flight of stairs she had to climb. During her last years Al had to carry her up and down the stairs to the attic. In 1971 Elizabeth suffered a heart attack and died. Grace refused to acknowledge her death.

During the Smouters' first year there, Grace suffered a stroke. She was bedridden and totally blind. She was entirely dependent on Al and Phipps described the situation well. "At times Grace seemed desperate and afraid and Al had to hold her hand and listen silently while she told stories of the Cawthras that he had heard countless times before. At times she was angry; eventually she stopped talking and eating and would let no one near her."

The Cawthra legacy must continue, but how? In her distress, Grace contacted Latham Burns, grandson to her brother Victor. She begged him to change his name to Cawthra; she tried to bribe him with the promise of sole inheritance, but he refused.

Phipps stated, "When he declined her offer she decided that she wasn't going to die. She would not write a will and would not talk about death." Instead, she tried harder to live in the past, believing that if the past refused to vanish she would remain as well. On October 22, 1974, Grace Cawthra died at the age of ninety-six. She was buried in the Dixie Union Chapel Cemetery at Cawthra and Dundas beside her late husband.

For years and years Grace believed she only had limited funds to cover her expenses. She slept on threadbare sheets, refusing to replace them. Lawyers for the estate later discovered a locked closet piled high with linens. When the vault in the basement was opened it was found to be filled with sterling silver. Her estate was valued at $1,719,675, not to mention the estimated worth of the home and property.

The City of Mississauga purchased the Cawthra Estate in 1975 for $2.6 million. The Smouters continued to care for the estate until 1977. Then the Porter family assumed the duties of caretaking. At the time, Mrs. Porter felt uneasy about living in the mansion. She was convinced that the estate was haunted. Journalist Alana Perkins wrote, "One attic window would not remain closed — no matter how many times Porter locked it. One day Mrs. Porter got angry and shouted 'Look, are you coming or going? Whatever you do, shut the window behind you.' Apparently she never had any problem locking the window after that.

"Mrs. Porter also once commented, 'I believe I've been touched by someone.'" Could it be Grace or Elizabeth?

Today the estate is used by the City of Mississauga as a training and conference facility. Although the home is closed to the public, the grounds can be enjoyed by one and all. Some Mississauga residents just visit the estate to gaze at the splendour of an old-growth forest, which still surrounds the house. You can be sure that some visitors to the Cawthra Estate feel uneasy, as if someone is watching them. This is certainly the case for the security staff of the City of Mississauga, who patrol the estate at night.

I arrived at the Cawthra Estate to meet Chris Harding, a young and friendly, albeit serious, employee of the city, whose job it is to provide security for the house and grounds. I had heard that Chris was sensitive to the paranormal energy that exists there.

Chris welcomed me and invited me into the mansion. We entered what would have been Grace's living room. It was my intention to question Chris about his experiences and to find out if Grace or any other spirits still lived here. It wasn't long before Chris began telling a story about a co-worker who also patrols this estate. He encountered a spirit outside the building one night.

"One of my co-workers was patrolling the estate at night. He pulled the car up near the side of the building. His car lights were reflecting off the wall. He got out of the car and began walking in front of the head-lights towards the mansion. He took notice of his shadow in the light, but out of the corner of his eye, he spied another shadow following him. He quickly turned around, but there was neither shadow nor person there. He decided to continue walking and see if he could catch sight of any-thing. Within moments the shadow reappeared this time bobbing along just to the side of him. Once again it vanished. The security officer had had enough. He walked back to his patrol car and left."

Chris is convinced that there is a spiritual presence in the building. "I've come here and felt an overwhelming sense of being watched by someone. I hear this inner voice stating that I should leave the premises. The upstairs is not the most pleasant place to be. The feeling of not being wanted is so intense here," stated Chris. This is the area where Grace's bedroom was located.

Near the centre hall on the second floor is a set of narrow stairs, leading to the attic. Elizabeth, the housekeeper lived here. For twenty years she called the attic home. The only evidence today that the attic was once living quarters is the existence of two rooms. The one room on the left would have been Elizabeth's bedroom and the other room a bathroom. The rest of the attic space is now used for storage.

Chris never likes going to the attic. In fact, he said "The attic is definitely a place where you get the feeling that you are invading some-one's privacy."

The daytime staff always turns off the lights and set the security sys-tem before leaving the premises. Chris said, "We have arrived on a few occasions and found the lights on at night. Every once in a while it will be a hallway light on. The lights always seem to be on during the Halloween festivities." Grace Cawthra died near the time of All Hallows Night.

On one occasion during a private gathering, some guests encountered some hostility from a spirit there.

"My girlfriend's sister-in-law had rented the building for a baby shower. My girlfriend, her mother, and her sister were on the main floor in the room to the left of the main entrance," stated Chris. This would have been the dining room.

Chris continued, "They had a long table set up and drinks and food placed on it. My girlfriend's mother was standing by the table when suddenly a cup rose up in the air and flew at her, splashing the drink down the front of her dress. Her sister watched the whole event unfold. The only comment the mother had to say was, 'Excuse me, do you mind?'"

Although Chris has yet to see Grace, or whoever else is still residing here, he knows he is never alone late at night, walking the hallways and rooms of the Cawthra Estate. He does admit that he often hears sounds in the house during his security check, but believes there must be some reasonable explanation. He only questions himself when he hears the creaking floors above echoing the footsteps of a person; this leaves him feeling quite unsettled.

One city employee I interviewed did admit to smelling a strange odour. The woman, who refused to give her name, works on the second floor of the house. On occasion she smells burning toast. I asked her if there was anything else. She said no, and then commented on needing to adjust her chair once in a while. Is there someone who likes to sit in her chair at night?

While researching this story, I encountered a very intuitive, astute, and perceptive clairvoyant by the name of John Carlos Perrone. Several people had mentioned his name to me. I contacted him in order to help clarify who was still occupying the Cawthra Estate from the past. Was it Grace, who was so adamant to remain; or Elizabeth, who had called the estate home for many years? Perhaps Harry had never left his beloved home and wife. I phoned John and asked for an appointment.

John was willing to meet with me and discuss my questions. He had recently toured the estate and did have the information I needed to finish the story.

When I met John in his office in Mississauga, he welcomed me with a firm handshake and pleasant smile. My first question was what is the difference between a clairvoyant and a psychic? He answered, "A psychic wants to be right. A good clairvoyant wants to be accurate, helpful, and healing.

"I once said to a woman I was reading that she had been married once. She immediately challenged me by stating, I was wrong because she had been married three times. I replied that the only husband she had ever loved was the first one. It turned out that her other two marriages had only lasted two to three months. What I was saying was that she only had one real loving marriage. She agreed."

I asked him when he first became aware of this gift to see the past and future.

He answered, "The earliest memory I have of awakening to this gift was age three or four. I recall being in the back seat of the car. We had just visited some friends of my parents. I looked at my mother and said it was too bad that her lady friend we had just seen was going to die next Wednesday. My family was horrified. Sure enough the next Wednesday the woman was dead.

"My grandfather was a clairvoyant. He could communicate telepathically. He would be at his house and suddenly I would hear him tell me he was coming over and to put the coffee on. A few minutes later he would enter our house.

"My powers seem to be getting stronger as I get older. I now have spirits speak to me in other languages that I cannot understand. I can see them, but sometimes they are opaque, or orbs of light; or flashes of light; or shadows; energy imprints of people or events. For example, I can see the impression of the person who lived in a particular setting or even see a murder taking place."

I felt quite reassured by now of John's skills, and asked specifically about the Cawthra Estate. What impressions had John picked up?

He responded, "My sense was, as I approached the house that the focal point of spirit activity was in the attic.

"As I entered the house I knew there was no Grace Cawthra present. This very gracious woman has moved on. However, there are remnants of her energy still lingering. Her high intellectual energy knew to move on after her death.

"Yet people are constantly calling on her. These lookers and gogglers are calling on her energy to return. This drains her. She feels drawn from the other dimension. These people are harassing her. This is wrong.

"As I toured the house I immediately picked up male and female energy. The male is the strongest.

"The glass-plated addition the City of Mississauga had added on to the house a few years ago has severely disturbed the energy of the house. I felt a vortex of energy wafting and disturbing the electro-magnetic field. The ground under the addition should not have been disturbed."

John then shared his experiences as he entered the second floor and began the hike up the narrow staircase that led to the attic.

"As I approached the top of the stairs the male spirit told me to get out of here. Like a child, this male presence began stomping his feet. The female spirit was standing nearby in the attic. She yelled to her male companion to stop his antics.

"She was dressed in an ankle-length grey dress that bunched at the waist with puffy shoulders. She wore an apron over the dress that was somewhat soiled. She appeared to be in her mid-thirties. She is a kind woman who is happy to do her job. She died right there in the attic."

The description matched that of Elizabeth, the loyal servant to Grace.

John added, "She doesn't like this male spirit energy in her space. This male is a relation who Grace had approached to inherit the estate. He is angry that I have identified him. He is getting really angry. He felt entitled to the property. He and Grace Cawthra had a disagreement concerning how she wanted things done. In his mind he knew he would outlive her. My feeling is he died before Grace and was unable to do the scheming he had envisioned.

"He is not a dangerous spirit, but a nasty person. He feels this is his house. He doesn't want anyone here.

"The female spirit still keeps the house in order. She loves the city employees who now work here. She also keeps the male spirit in line."

This ended our session together. It would seem that John was able to shed some additional light on the spirit world of the Cawthra Estate.

The haunting of Cawthra may very well be about attachment. The inability to let go can result in imprisonment beyond this dimensional realm. Imagine the curse of attachment to something you never possessed in the first place. Letting go gets even more essential for us all, doesn't it?

The Eileen Sonin Story

~ Mississauga, Ontario ~

Do not place a mirror directly facing your bed. The mirror attracts wandering spirits who come to steal your consciousness.

WHEN I DISCOVERED THAT A FAMOUS MEDIUM ONCE LIVED IN Mississauga, Ontario, I was excited to learn more. As I became familiar with the life of Eileen Sonin, I felt saddened that I missed meeting this gifted seer. Her personal experiences completely confirmed for me the existence of spirits visiting us on the ethereal plane. Here is an abridged version of her life story:

Eileen Sonin was well-known for her stage, radio and television careers, but her true fame came from her abilities as a natural medium.

Born in Britain, Eileen left her homeland in 1957 to settle in Toronto and then Mississauga.

Her adventures into the unknown just happened. She never invited the experiences. "These strange events just happened to me; I did not seek them out and, in fact for many years, I believed that everyone at some time or other met with ghosts or had a glimpse into the future.

"Only when I came to Toronto, Canada, did I tell one of my 'ghost stories' in public and since that day, I have talked on all the entertainment media and lectured and written on this fascinating subject."

Eileen's journey into the spirit world began when she was eight years old. On that occasion she dreamed of seeing a child about her own age, running down a steep grassy hill. She described the girl, her hair streaming behind her in the wind. Flowers of a size and perfume never grown on this earth were strung around her neck, and she wore a tunic off one shoulder, in some semi-transparent material.

Eileen was so enthralled with this dream she would envision the delightful girl at her side whenever she was alone and eventually her dream-friend materialized into reality.

"I was fully aware that no one but myself could see her; I eventually treated her like a living child and we played splendid games together."

Eileen was a delicate child and remained at home. Together she and her invisible playmate shared the poems that Eileen wrote. "She even helped me to write plays for us both to act," said Eileen.

Eileen often wondered if she was dreaming all of this. She once asked her friend if she was real or invented. "She gave me such a pinch that I was convinced."

Then Eileen won a leading part in a play which was to tour England, Ireland, Scotland, and Wales. "We bade one another a tearful farewell, and although I looked for her on my return nearly a year later I never saw her again."

When Eileen lived in a village on the southwest coast of England, she became acquainted with an old woman known by the neighbourhood children as the "Witch of the Wood."

The "witch" was an eccentric old lady who eked out a living selling the herbs she grew and cheese that she made from the milk of her two goats. This elderly woman lived in a tumble-down, thatched hut with her large black cat.

One day Eileen and some friends were passing the witch's abode when they heard frightful yells and screeches. The children drew nearer. They discovered that some of the village youths had caught the witch's black cat, had tied a strong cord around its neck and another cord with a tin can to the cat's tail. They had then fastened both cords to the bottom rungs of the wooden gate.

Eileen saw that the village boys were firing stones at the immobilized animal. The poor cat had began to bleed from a stone to the head and it was screaming in terror. Eileen responded to the situation by lunging at the boys. Unable to manage them just by kicking, scratching, and hair-pulling, Eileen ended up on the ground with three boys hovering over her.

The timely arrival of the witch soon put an end to the whole affair. A few whacks from her garden rake put the youths to flight. As they untied the cat together the witch turned to Eileen and spoke. "Come and have a glass of milk, dearie. You are dusty and your dress is all torn."

Eileen recalled the moment, "I realized it was the witch who had made me the offer and, with a scream, I made off as fast as my legs would carry me, crying over my shoulder as I ran. 'No, no, you will turn me into gingerbread!'"

Eileen had no idea at the time that her act of compassion and goodwill towards the witch's black cat would later save her own life. A few months after the incident, Eileen went swimming with her friend Bethina. Eileen was ten years old at the time. After a leisurely swim Bethina insisted they explore the minework further along the beach. This was an area where no one was permitted to go — not even adults. It was here that there were long-disused passages and pits running inland under the towering cliffs where workers had mined massive slabs of granite to later be used in the construction of buildings in London. The girls followed the tracks to where the small underground railway had once transported the slabs from the mine. When they reached the mine, Bethina entered. Not wishing to appear frightened, Eileen followed. They travelled deeper and deeper into the mine. They followed one path, then another until they stood in total darkness.

Eileen exclaimed, "Stop, I don't like it here."

She demanded that they turn around and go back. Bethina immediately grabbed Eileen's arm and began pulling her along a path to the right of where they were standing. Eileen resisted. She declared the way out was the other direction. Bethina tugged her hand loose from Eileen's and was gone.

Now Eileen was extremely frightened. In fact, she was frozen with terror. Then she glimpsed a flash of light — it was the Witch of the Wood! Eileen called to Bethina. There was no reply. The witch beckoned Eileen to follow her. Eileen added, "She must have been carrying a small lantern or some light as I could see her quite clearly in the darkness."

She followed the witch up slopes and down corridors until they reached daylight. Eileen recalled, "Not even stopping to thank the witch, I tore home as fast as my legs could carry me to tell my mother, between breathless sobs, that Bethina was lost in the mines."

A search party set out to find Bethina. Sadly, she was discovered lying at the bottom of a shaft — dead!

When Eileen was questioned by the authorities, she explained that the witch had arrived and led her out of the mine. The village policeman told Eileen that was impossible. The witch had taken ill the week before and had died last Wednesday. Eileen stuck to her story and described the plaid shawl the old lady had worn over her shoulder.

The doctor confirmed that the witch had been wearing a very old, plaid shawl around her when she was discovered dead the week before.

Eileen later realized, "I had seen her as clearly as in life, with the yellow glow of light around her which I had taken to be a lantern. I have always liked to think that she came to repay the debt which she felt she owed me for my defence of the cat."

Eileen added, "Since that day I took old Satan (the black cat) home to live out the rest of his life with us, any and every cat will come if I call. Also, a gypsy fortune teller told me quite recently that I had the power of the evil eye, that is, I could ill-wish anyone. A coincidence? I think not."

Eileen eventually married an English journalist, Ray Sonin, in 1938. Ray, on September 13, 1958, launched a successful Canadian career in radio, on CFRB Toronto, with a show entitled "Calling all Britons."

From her book entitled *Ghosts I have Known*, Eileen shared a ghostly encounter in the home they first occupied together as a married couple. The dwelling was located on 51 Peel Street, Kensington, England. It was described by Eileen as "a pretty, little doll's house of a place." According to her, "The house had two small living rooms downstairs, one facing front and [the] other opening out from it to make a dining room. Directly facing the front door, at the end of the narrow passage, was the kitchen and above it the bathroom, then a few stairs up to the bedrooms, one over each of the two living rooms.

"The front of the roof had two gables like two capital 'A's' with a strip dividing them, running from front to back and down on to the lower level of the flat roof over the kitchen\bathroom addition. This flat roof carried the tank which supplied the house with its water. I have taken the time to describe the layout of the place because it is essential to my story."

Eileen and Ray had been in the house just a little more than two weeks when Ray left for Scotland on business for three days. Being a young bride, Eileen set to work fixing the house up as soon as Ray left. It was near midnight when she and her two cats retired upstairs to bed.

Just as Eileen entered that pleasant state of half-awake, half-asleep, she was awakened with a jolt by the sounds of heavy footsteps on the roof. Eileen described the activity. "I knew it was a man at once and that he was wearing heavy boots by the way the grit and dirt crunched under his feet. 'A burglar,' was my first thought, but he was not making the slightest attempt to keep quiet."

Eileen made a mental note of the time. It was 12:35 a.m. Then the footsteps ceased. At exactly 3:35 a.m., the footsteps returned from the opposite direction.

The next day Eileen attempted to dismiss the activities of the previous night. Once again she worked all day in the house and retired late. Then at 12:35 a.m. the footsteps came again.

"My imagination spun such terrifying stories that I made no attempt to sleep and huddled with the bedclothes up to my chin waiting for 3:35 a.m. and what I was now convinced would be the return journey. Sure enough, he walked again."

When Ray returned Eileen poured out her story about the man on the roof. That night at the same time Ray heard the footsteps. He followed the sound of the steps with his eyes. He took notice that the two cats awakened from sleep and sat up prior to he and Eileen hearing the footsteps.

"That's a ghost!" declared Ray emphatically. "Those steps just could not be any human feet."

Ray explained to Eileen that the footsteps went diagonally across the roof in a way that would be humanly impossible as the person would have to climb up and down the two sloping roofs to get from point A to point B, and his measured tread proved that he was not doing any climbing.

Eileen still felt the footsteps belonged to an intruder. The police were phoned the next morning. Eventually two men from the Criminal Investigation Department (CID) were assigned to the case. The two officers staked the house out prior to midnight.

They decided to hide behind the water tank on the roof. Disappointment prevailed. The burglar or phantom-walker never appeared. They heard nothing.

The next night the detectives returned. This time one officer joined Eileen and Ray in the bedroom. The other officer positioned himself downstairs ready to dash out and climb up onto the roof the moment he heard the signal from his partner. It was arranged that a knock on the floor would indicated the sound of footsteps on the roof.

Right on time, 12:35 a.m., the footsteps could be heard. The officer knocked on the floor and dashed downstairs to join his partner and nab the suspect. The men saw nothing. For two weeks they chased the phantom footsteps without success.

According to Eileen, "They covered the roof with flour and although we all heard the footsteps, the flour was not disturbed. They tied black cotton backwards and forwards, criss-crossing the entire roof, yet it remained unbroken."

The Sonins held ghost parties and as many as twenty people at a time sat up in their bedroom and waited for the man to walk across the roof.

On one occasion the man slipped. Eileen explained, "It sounded as if he was carrying a sack full of small round objects. They rolled in all directions, making a terrible noise all over the roof.

"He, himself, did not seem to fall. It was just as if he had missed his footing and had dropped whatever he had been carrying. I always thought they sounded like old-fashioned brass doorknobs."

By now they had begun to feel the extreme cold, which filled the room before they would hear the sound of the man walking. The detectives decided to research the history of the house. They soon discovered that, during the construction of the building, a workman had fallen from the roof scaffolding and been killed.

Eileen added, "This, of course, explained how our 'man on the roof' was able to walk diagonally across. It was before the gables had been put on. He was walking on the roof supports."

The detectives finally agreed that the walker on the roof came from some other world. And so it was that in the records at the Kensington Police Station, the Sonin home, number 51 Peel Street, is described as a haunted house.

While still residing in England, Eileen went to visit Madame Viera, a fortune teller. Eileen described her visit, "She told me many things, most of which I have forgotten, but one thing I do recall. She said I would travel a long distance across water and start an entirely new life in another country. This I thought was quite ridiculous as both Ray and I were established in our careers, earning comfortable salaries, and we owned our own house in London as well as a cottage in the country.

"And yet, a few years later we were to sell up and come out to Canada on an impulse to an absolutely new and wonderful life."

At the end of the session Eileen asked Madame Viera how much she owed her for the reading. Madame Viera replied, "I couldn't take money from you. The spirits would be very cross. You have so many spirits guarding you that I could not risk offending them."

From the winnings of a football pool Eileen and Ray purchased a charming property in East Anglia. It was a sizeable house with a thatched roof located on the borders of the village of Southolt and Worlingworth. The nearby town of Eay had castle ruins and an old monastery. The Sonins named their new home Forthingale.

Eileen was quite drawn to the two elder trees growing near the house. "In these parts, you will invariably find an elder planted near the old cottages — some relic from the Druids or a heathen charm against being struck by lightning, I was told. Even now it is considered bad luck by the locals to cut them down."

One evening Eileen's cat Miranda crouched on the window sill and began to growl. Eileen rose from her chair and walked over to the window to investigate.

"Peering out into the dusk, at first I saw nothing, but then, standing under the elder tree quite close to the house, I saw a figure.

"It was a man in monk's habit and he just stood looking up at the tree with mist swirling around him quite thickly. On no other part of the grounds could I see any mist. I noticed that the folds of his black habit, which looked worn and shabby, hung as they would from human shoulders and I tapped on the window to attract his attention. He turned slowly towards me, looked up at the elder tree, and then gently shook his head, almost as if admonishing me for something. Then, lifting the hem of his robe with one hand he walked down towards the bottom of our field and vanished. To my knowledge there were no monks in our district."

When Ray returned, Eileen shared her story about the appearance of the monk.

Eileen's story continued. "Ray seemed interested in the monk. 'You say he stood under the elder,' he said.

"'Yes,' I replied."

"Ray murmured half to himself. 'Black habit?' Yes."

"Ray added, 'Well, this morning I talked it over with old George, (George was our handyman) and we decided between us to cut down that elder.'"

Eileen became quite adamant that this would not happen. She announced to Ray, "That is why the monk shook his head. He was telling me not to let you cut it down."

The colour, worn by the Benedictine Monks, was black and their house had formerly been the property of the Benedictine Order. What Eileen had witnessed was the ghost of one of those holy men.

Her book entitled *Canadian Ghosts*, written in 1970, highlighted numerous ghost stories from across Canada. In the book Eileen makes reference to the "ever-widening group of people who are aware of some of the wonders the mind can achieve, from a thought contact with the living, to a vision of those who have gone before and who wait for us on another plane where the soul survives and the spirit is everlasting."

Eileen was well aware of the great writers and poets, such as Sir Oliver Lodge, Professor Huxley, Edgar Cayce, Camille Flammarion and Jean-Jacques Rosseau. She said, "They all stated their interest and belief in cosmic consciousness and the survival of man's soul, who are we to doubt? Many have left their discoveries and writings as signposts along the way to help those who would follow and bring more enlightened thought to bear upon this vast subject. If I sound as if I am preaching, I am, for I firmly believe that, the more we know about the etheric, the better lives we lead and the happier we become."

In her book, Eileen briefly explained how she saw ghosts. "I see ghosts in two ways. Sometimes they look as if they are living persons and I see them with my physical eye; at other times I see them mentally. It is as if I suddenly know or am told what they look like and why they are there."

In 1972, historian Kathleen Hicks interviewed Eileen for her weekly column in the *News*, entitled "A VIP and Me." Kathleen asked Eileen, "What sensitivities do you feel you have that enable you to detect the presence of a ghost or spirit?"

Eileen answered, "I experience a peculiar feeling, it's kind of a cold feeling down the back of my neck, and a funny sensation in my head. It's very hard to explain or put into words, but it is an awareness.

"When I walk into a house, I know whether there are spirits inhabiting it or not. When something happens that gives me some insight that I have to tell somebody, I don't think it first, I just say it; and when I say it, I hear if for the first time. It's talking without thinking in a way, because there's no positive thought that directed the speech. It's like being in a trance, but I'm awake."

Kathleen then asked Eileen if she minded being christened the "Ghost Lady" after having arrived in Canada and having had a television debut.

"No, not at all."

"You have a difficult task set forth for you. Tell me how you feel about informing people about the supernatural," enquired Kathleen.

"I went to England two years ago and consulted various people who tell you your future. Ena Twigg, who is world famous, told me I had a job to do, that I had to explain to people about the supernatural. This is really my lot in life. I have to let people know that if they have experiences, they shouldn't be afraid; that's the most important thing of all. They should accept them. People are more open and ready to accept things today, especially the youngsters; they seem to be particularly fascinated by the subject.

"I was also told that I should write as well, which of course I have been doing."

"And you don't have to be a crank or peculiar to believe as I do and as Shakespeare did, that 'there are more things in heaven and earth ... than are dreamt of in your philosophy'. All these aspects of my life I find extremely rewarding."

Another subject of strong belief for Eileen was reincarnation. She recalled once living as a woman during the French Revolution where she was carted away to the guillotine and executed. A second life was recalled in ancient Greece. Once again she was sacrificed.

In her book *Canadian Ghosts*, she described a couple who had lost their two daughters in an automobile accident. A year or so later the couple had twin girls born to them. Eileen described what happened next, "As the girls started to talk, the parents noticed that, when left alone, they called each other by the names of the two dead girls, who incidentally, were not twins."

The parents became quite alarmed and consulted their family doctor. He advised them that on no account must the accident ever be discussed in front of the twins.

"However, whenever the girls believed themselves to be unobserved they talked about the car smash, exchanging reminiscences about their feelings at the time, and they persisted in using the names of the dead sisters," added Eileen.

The real proof that the twins were indeed their lost daughters came when the family went to visit the home of a distant relative, where the twins had never previously visited.

"The last few miles of the journey were filled with shouts of joy from the girls as they recognized various landmarks. On arrival at the house they needed no guidance to make their way at once to the bedroom which had been occupied by the dead sisters on their only visit to the place.

"What is more, they amazed the family by excitedly asking if the rose wallpaper was still there because they had liked it so much.

"During the vacation, they gave so much evidence that they knew the house and the surroundings that it became obvious to the family that the knowledge they possessed could only have been gained by their having been there before." The parents were forced to draw the conclusion that they had indeed a reincarnation of their two dead daughters in the twins."

In November of 1977, Eileen Sonin left this earthly plane to begin a new journey. Her husband remarried and lived until August of 1991.

Perhaps Eileen is back living amongst us. If that should be the case I trust that this time around she'll make sure I meet up with her. "How about it, Eileen?"

Cherry Hill House

~ Mississauga, Ontario ~

IT IS EARLY 1900. A GROUP OF SPIRITUALISTS ARE SECRETLY GATHERED IN a private location to share a ritual. They want to connect with their dead relatives or friends. Most participants are impassioned about, perhaps even obsessed with, exploring this unknown realm. Their imaginations are keen, not necessarily reasoned. They sit around the table, arms outstretched, guided by a Shakespearean actor who instructs them to lightly rest their hands on a heart-shaped object in the centre of a homemade Ouija board. A single candle, flickering on the pine mantelpiece, casts eerie shadows about the room.

They begin, "Spirit, if you are there, give us a sign." The movable pointer quickly slides to the word "yes."

"Do you have a name?" The pointer flies around the alphabet to spell, "Two Feathers."

"Why are you here?" A sudden gust of wind in the room causes the candle flame to cast ominous shadows around the room. The candle goes out. The participants flee in terror. Will the spirit remain?

Here we are in 2013, many years and perhaps, many spirits later. We are at Cherry Hill House.

Built by Joseph Silverthorn, it is the oldest surviving house in Mississauga. Joseph was a United Empire Loyalist who married fifteen-year-old Jane Chisholm in Queenston Heights in April of 1807 and moved to what is now Mississauga. There he built a six-metre by four-metre cabin where they lived in harmony with the Ojibwa who wandered through the area in small groups, hunting and fishing. They recorded how the Native Peoples often visited, walking into the cabin unannounced to sit and watch them silently. Initially this was alarming to Jane, especially when Joseph was away.

By 1815 Joseph had begun construction of a stately home, built with his own trees and with fieldstone gathered from a nearby stream, later called Etobicoke Creek. This magnificent structure was completed by 1822.

Joseph and Jane planted a mile of cherry trees from the front gate to the barn, encircling the homestead and inspiring the name "Cherry Hill" for the estate. These were cherry trees originally brought to New Jersey from an ancestral home in England by Oliver Silverthorn in 1700. Joseph maintained the tradition when he brought young saplings from that home to his new estate.

The Silverthorns had twelve children; nine daughters and three sons. One child died at birth. They were among the first white children to be born in Toronto Township.

The Cherry Hill House, 1815

On July 12, 1879, Joseph passed away, leaving Jane and three daughters, Augusta, Jane and Helen, to manage the estate. Jane died in November of the same year. By 1907 Augusta was the sole owner of Cherry Hill. On December 10 of that year she passed away, leaving the estate to her favourite nephew, William Stanislas Romain.

William was an actor, a dramatic artist, and a vocalist, who trained in England and began his career at age eighteen. William was considered to be quite an eccentric; he dressed oddly, perhaps due to his profession, which he took seriously. He acted in many countries where he worked alongside talented people such as Sarah Bernhardt and Mary Pickford. He was also drawn to spiritualism. Kathleen Hicks, author and historian, has spent the last few years compiling a book about the Silverthorn family and Cherry Hill House. Kathleen was important in the movement to save the building from demolition in 1973.

Kathleen wrote, "Mr. Romain apparently didn't appreciate his inheritance, for it was after he took over the Silverthorn homestead that the house was let go to gradual ruin. William rented parts of the house to several families, while he maintained a section of the house for himself. In the early 1950s, a friend of the family, Miss Lindsay, rented the home. William died, at the age of eighty-four, in 1951."

Unfortunately, most of his tenants felt that William was responsible for repairs.

Kathleen added, "The house gradually deteriorated, until the front veranda was down, and a grey pallor clung to the unpainted interior." In 1973, the home was threatened with demolition until a group of concerned citizens and a developer moved the house from its original location at the corner of Dundas Street and Cawthra. It now stands a few hundred yards away at 680 Silvercreek Boulevard.

The house was completely renovated and restored to its original grandeur by the Triomphe Group. Perhaps it was fitting that the house opened to the public on the eve of Halloween, 1979, as the Cherry Hill House Restaurant.

Kathleen wrote, "William held elaborate parties in the driving shed and he and his guests would dress as Shakespearean characters." She also wrote about his spiritualism and the séances at Cherry Hill House. We can only speculate about the results of those activities.

For years, stories have circulated about the haunting of Cherry Hill House. The appearance of any dilapidated old house will conjure up spooky images in many minds. Whispers begin and before you know it, it becomes the gospel truth. However, these haunting were documented.

The first account, written by Frank Jones and entitled "Visiting Our Restless Spirits," appeared in the *Toronto Star* on October 26, 1980. The first reported sighting occurred in 1973, before the house was moved, according to Mr. Jones. "In that year, a security guard, Ron Land, was sitting outside the deserted house guarding it one night when he saw a white figure rise out of a pile of earth, brandishing a sword. Land jumped out of his car, and his dog, Cindy, ran towards the figure. The dog shied away, and as the figure came towards him, Land, too, turned and fled. Police kept watch the next night but saw nothing."

Could this apparition that rose from the soil be a spirit, lingering from a séance half a century ago?

After the house was moved down the street, another security guard witnessed the unbelievable. He saw a girl, dressed in white, sitting on a white horse inside the house. On another occasion a medium, who was dining at the restaurant, reported that the girl wearing white was the spirit of a sixteen year old. Her name was Miranda and she burned to death in the house while making candles. According to Kathleen Hicks, there was never a Silverthorn named Miranda, nor any mention of a fire in the house. It may be that a girl by this name resided in the house during the years that William had tenants.

Reports of Native apparitions and rumours about Native burial grounds have circulated and been documented by writers, including John Robert Columbo. These include accounts of old Native faces floating out of the fireplace, workmen's tools disappearing, and bizarre accidents on stairs.

Kathleen Hicks maintains that Cherry Hill was never constructed on top of a Native burial ground. However, some people believe the foundation blocks came from a nearby field that was once used as an Indian burial site.

Once again, Ms. Hicks helped to clarify this by adding, "The stones used during the construction of the house were transported by Joseph Silverthorn himself from the Etobicoke Creek to the property." Although there is a Native presence in the building, it is, in her estimations, in no way related to a burial ground.

Anita is a young woman who worked as a bartender and was the supervisor of the Duke of Marlborough, an authentic British pub located on the lower level of Cherry Hill House Restaurant. The pub is quaint, with its flagstone floor and fireplace at the far end. A bar with a few stools is situated to the right of the main entrance and a short corridor leads to the washrooms and to a flight of stairs up to the first floor. Anita had heard stories from friends about hauntings at Cherry Hill before she worked there as an employee. These stories primarily centered on a presence in the attic of the building. Naturally, she had no idea that her first day on the job would reveal some truth about those stories.

Anita is an experienced waitress, focused on her work and very capable. Nonetheless, on her first day at the job she had an accident. "I was carrying a tray of drinks to a table and fell. Something tripped me. I turned around but nothing was there. I am superstitious and felt I needed to respond in some way. So a week later I went up to the attic and spoke to the spirits. I said, 'Please leave me alone. I like you and mean no harm to you.'"

Her next encounter happened when she found someone standing just a few feet away from her. "It was 10:30 p.m. There were two or three customers sitting at the bar. I was in the process of pouring a drink when I caught sight of a figure out of the corner of my eye. Right at the doorway of the storage room and not far from the bar was a Native man. He was tall, about six feet, four inches, and was wearing light beige deerskin. I could also see his deerskin leggings. He had long, dark-brown hair. He could have been in his thirties. I turned quickly to get a better look at him and he was gone."

On another occasion a husband, wife, and mother-in-law arrived for an evening meal. They were seated on the first floor, in front of the fireplace. In the middle of a conversation, the older woman suddenly caught a glimpse of a Native woman by the fireplace. She questioned what she was seeing, but no one else could see the woman.

The staff has seen an old Native man floating in mid-air or walking down the stairs. One worker felt a hand grip his shoulder. When he turned around he saw the elderly Native standing behind him. Then the Native man vanished.

Anita is certain that spirits inhabit Cherry Hill. In fact she had several different experiences, especially after closing time. "I often heard footsteps on the first floor situated above the pub. One minute the footsteps are above the bar on the main floor and the next minute you could hear them at the other end of the pub. The footsteps are heard on a regular basis.

"One night after closing the pub, about 2:00 a.m., I put the radio on to help me get in motion. As I left the bar to wipe the first table, the radio turned off. I walked back and as soon as I turned the corner of the bar the radio came back on. This happened to me four times. I had had enough, closed up and left the building."

On another occasion, shortly after closing time, Anita and her boyfriend experienced the very disconcerting sound of a hissing cat. They left quickly.

Anna Maria and Guerrino Staropoli took over Cherry Hill House Restaurant in 1985 from the Triomphe chain. Guerrino related an experience that happened to him when they first began operating the business. "I was working late one night in the office located on the second floor when I heard two knocks." He thought the knocking was coming from the hallway outside the office door. Then he realized it was actually within the wall that separated the office from another room.

Apparitions frequently appear near the fireplace.

The stairway to the attic is also located in the office area. Guerrino remembers an incident when friends were seated in the main floor dining area on the right hand side of the building. The diners were the only ones in the room. Suddenly one of the wall lights near their table began to flash on and off while the other lights in the room remained on.

A previous owner of Cherry Hill Restaurant reported that when he closed up at night he would make sure all the lights were off before leaving the building. As he was driving away he would often catch sight of a light on in the attic window of the building. He would return to the restaurant, go up the stairs to the attic and turn the light off; yet the moment he would drive away the light would come on again!

Alicia was another long-term employee of the Cherry Hill House Restaurant, a waitress there from 1985 to 1996. She actually walked right through one of the spirits. "My first experience was when I was waitressing in the pub. It was at about 9:00 p.m. when I took a short break and went to the ladies' washroom. As I was leaving the washroom I walked right through what seemed to be a fog. The fog was actually in the shape of a human. It was very tall and large. My body was shaking and felt extremely cold when I walked through it. I returned to the bar and shared my experience with the bartender.

"On another occasion, I was serving two girls seated at a table by the fireplace. One girl looked at me and quivered. The other girl said, 'Is there a ghost here?' Her friend was visibly shaken and was feeling cold. Apparently, she was very sensitive and felt the presence of a spirit. They quickly left the pub."

Alicia is certain that the spirits in the house have never harmed anyone; in fact, they are quite pleasant. One evening she was alone counting the cash. "My back was turned to the seating area in the pub. I felt someone was watching me. I was scared in the beginning, but I got used to it. The same thing happens when you go upstairs to the office late at night. You can feel a presence."

Some incidences are extraordinary phenomena. "The power had gone out and we lit some candles for light in the restaurant. I went outside to see the whole neighbourhood in darkness, including the restaurant. As I walked around to the back of the building I looked up and to my amazement a light was on in every window of the attic.

Someone was there!" It would seem the spirits have their own source of electricity!

Music is another way in which spirits express themselves. Some spiritualists believe that all thought ultimately expresses itself through sound. This sound is often described as a series of ever-changing chords, "as of a thousand Eolian harps." Angels are considered to be a class of spirits who are devoted to music and who habitually express themselves this way. Late one night in the pub Alicia heard just such a sound. "I knew the radio was off. When I walked by the radio speakers I could hear music coming from them. It was the most heavenly music I have ever heard."

I felt Alicia was a "sensitive." She told me, "When I was a child, my grandmother died. About two weeks after her death I was sleeping with my mother when I suddenly awakened. My dead grandmother had appeared and walked to the bedside where my mother was sleeping. My mother's arm was hanging over the side of the bed. My grandmother took my mother's hand and held it. Then she moved back towards the wall and disappeared."

If a mother is a "sensitive," her daughter may have the same abilities. Similarly, mothers and daughters can have a deep psychic bond. Energy and psychic awareness are often awakened when someone dies. When the physical body goes and only energy remains, some of that energy may be gifted by the mother to her daughter, a true psychic legacy.

In 2005, a group of dinner guests at the Cherry Hill Restaurant became aware that an elderly woman in their group was turned towards the fireplace and engaged in an animated conversation. The guests exchanged glances, with their eyebrows raised, because they did not understand what she was doing. When questioned she replied, "I was having a conversation with the woman in the rocking chair by the fireplace." None of them could see either a woman or a rocking chair.

In 2006, Anna Maria and Guerrino Staropoli retired from the restaurant business and sold to Parvinder Chandi, who continued the tradition of fine dining at Cherry Hill Restaurant.

The restaurant took a new direction in 2010. Maureen Scott, in an article entitled "Victoria's Gluton Free Bistro" writes in the *Goodlife Magazine*, "Necessity is the mother of invention. When two people in a family of restaurateur, discovered they had a gluten allergy and could no longer enjoy pizza and pasta, they decided to open their own gluten-free restaurant.

"The gluten-free bistro concept was the brainchild of Mickey and Arlene Vesia.

"We have two separate kitchens — one which is 100 percent gluten free with waiters who only serve from the gluten-free kitchen so there can be no cross contamination."

They changed the name of the restaurant to Victoria's Gluten-Free Bistro. The downstairs pub was renamed the Cherry Hill Pub.

Margo Marshall is the bar manager of the establishment. She has worked there for the past sixteen years. She is well aware of the hauntings in the building. "After all these years, people are still hearing and seeing things in the restaurant.

"A young girl, who worked here about six months ago, came by one day to pick up her pay cheque. She had left her three-year-old son in the car. She quickly rushed into the building. In the meantime, the young boy experienced a visitation while sitting in the car. A little girl appeared on the front porch of the restaurant and began to talk to the boy. When the mother returned to the vehicle, the son told his mother about the girl. The mother looked up at the porch, but could not see any little girl."

Margo Marshall, bar manager. An orb of light appears in the top right section of the ceiling.

A few years ago, during a Halloween costume party in the pub, a couple were having dinner in the upstairs restaurant. At one point the male diner left and went to the washroom. While standing at the urinal, the gentleman suddenly felt as though someone were watching him. According to Margo, "He turned around and saw a Native man, dressed in traditional clothing, behind him. The customer did not appreciate this man watching him, at that moment in time. He complained to the management. Anna Marie, the owner at the time, went downstairs to the pub to inquire if there was any one at the party dressed as a Native. There was no such costume at the party."

When Mickey and Arlene took over the business they began some interior renovations. Apparently one spirit was not too pleased. Margo said, "A psychic would occasionally drop in to the restaurant. During this time he told me that Joseph Silverthorn was unhappy with the renovations to the building.

"On another occasion the same psychic arrived and was seated at the downstairs bar. During this time he kept looking at the wall by the bar. I asked him what he was looking at. He replied, 'There are three entities in the bar. One is by the wall and the other two are by you. The spirits near you are protecting you.' Afterwards he asked if he could go upstairs and tour the restaurant, which was under renovations. We went upstairs and as we reached the bar he said, 'I have to leave, the spirits are angry with me.' I have never seen him since."

Margo tells a story about what happened to some workers during the renovations to the building.

"The workers had an MP3 player connected to the stereo system. One day it vanished and was never seen again."

Margo added, "People come here because they believe in the spirit world."

It would seem to be a need or a curiosity for a spiritual experience, for many of these visitors, but what about Margo?

"I do believe. Strange things have happened here — things being moved around. One time in the morning, before opening up, I was at the bar. I heard footsteps where the old stairs use to be leading up to the bar."

Late one night Margo had a very unusual experience in the building; she thought she was all alone!

"I was in the downstairs pub, closing up the bar. It was 2:30 a.m. I suddenly heard what sounded like a table being tipped over in the upstairs dining room. I heard the cutlery landing on the floor. At that time the upstairs was all locked up."

Margo did not go to investigate.

"I was off work the next day, but I phoned to ask the maître d' if he had noticed anything unusual in the dining room. He replied, 'A dining room table had been turned over and the glasses broken!'"

The many and varied accounts of spiritual activity in the building would seem to indicate several spirits continue to inhabit Cherry Hill House. There is activity in the attic and in the office located at the base of the attic staircase. Customers have seen a spirit on the main floor, as well as in the pub. Several different spirits have been seen, including the white figure rising up out of the earth brandishing a sword; a girl wearing white riding a horse inside the building; a tall Native man wearing buckskins in the pub; an old Native man appearing in the attic; a Native girl standing by the fireplace on the first floor of the restaurant; a young girl on the porch; a hissing cat, and even the sound of heavenly music. They include angels and saints who are not caught on this plane but are attendant here to help those in need of them.

This is a tremendous amount of activity for one building; did William Stanislas Romain create some kind of spirit corridor here when he invited spirits in through his séances?

You may judge for yourself when you visit the Cherry Hill House, now known as Victoria's Gluten-Free Bistro.

The Blue Elephant Restaurant
~ Simcoe, Ontario ~

If a woman is buried in black she will return to haunt the family.

THE YEAR IS 1915. A YOUNG VIBRANT CANADIAN WOMAN OF CLEAR, white complexion is strolling hand-in-hand down a tree-lined street with her American lover. He gazes at her and studies her fine features. Her long auburn hair, tied back in a ponytail, helps accentuate her youth. Her slight frame allows the white chiffon dress to flow gracefully, yet not hide her delicate features.

He squeezes her hand as they near her place of residence, an ornate nineteenth-century red brick storey-and-a-half structure. Once a single family residence, it now serves as a rooming house.

It is time for him to take his leave and return to his American home. Their only future means of communication will be letters.

For a woman in her mid-twenties, courtship and marriage meant salvation; but, fate dealt her a losing hand. The grim reaper had moved in down the hallway, just biding his time.

The Blue Elephant Restaurant, late 1800s.

Months went by before death struck. Her spirit was released — or was it taken? It would seem however, that love can reach out from beyond the grave. She has returned to await her lover ... and she is not the only spirit to return in this place.

Welcome to her home, now the Blue Elephant Restaurant, in downtown Simcoe, Ontario.

Heather Pond, a passionate and caring individual, took ownership of the building in 1992. Heather's intention was to operate a restaurant. Fortunately for her, the setting had already been transformed into a fine dining establishment back in 1979. The Spencer family built the home in the late 1800s and became a rooming house in the early 1900s. John Allen Barholom took ownership on February 5, 1924. John and his wife Martha Tiffany raised two daughters there; these daughters never married and they lived together in the house after their parents died. One sister, Gladys, became a music teacher and turned part of the house into a conservatory where she taught music until her death in the 1970s. She initially used a room on the second floor for teaching and, later in her life, moved the music lessons to the first floor.

Heather is familiar with, and readily acknowledges, the spirit world. She is one of those extraordinary people who have the ability to access another dimension of reality that is invisible to most of us. Heather can see spirits when they relate to her own personal surroundings, such as seeing her deceased grandparents at home.

Heather has always worked in the food and beverage business. Her restaurant is important to her and this is reflected in the decor and in the loyalty of many of her staff who have remained with her since the early days of her ownership. The community of Simcoe is actually her hometown.

The existence of the young woman who boarded there back in the early 1900s was substantiated by the discovery of her intimate letters to her American lover, found during renovations in the 1980s. Unfortunately Heather has not yet received copies of those letters and has only an oral accounting of them.

"How do we know she is still here?" You may ask.

Heather has seen her!

She described one of her experiences to me.

"I feel a lot of cold drafts upstairs in the building. I have seen the light — it is her, looking very majestic, very white. I can recognize her features. I see eyes, and her mouth. She looks like a porcelain doll. Her frame is thin and she always wears her hair in a ponytail. She wears a long chiffon dress while walking the hallways."

She also appears on the first floor, but is never seen past the steps by the bathroom leading into the pub area, which was added on to the building in 1987.

A room that was once Heather's office is now a new micro brewery with two brands of beer.

Heather confirmed, "I saw her in my old office until it was moved to the new part of the building."

This female spirit actually smiles at Heather when they meet.

Heather says, "I sense she approves of what I am doing with the restaurant and loves to see the people who dine and drink here."

Nevertheless, there is something about her that seems sad or confused.

Heather explains, "I think she is lost. It is as if she is in a time warp. Every time we change something around here she makes her presence known."

Smell is often associated with the presence of spirits, such as perfume or tobacco smoke. Heather often notes a sweet smell in the restaurant.

This female spirit is also playful, according to Heather. On a number of occasions staff members have arrived at work in the morning to discover a particular picture sitting on the floor, leaning against the wall. Finally they agreed to just eliminate that picture in the dining room.

One Christmas, Heather had purchased two corn angel dolls, as part of the decorations. She hung the two angels on the dining room wall. Once again there was some objection from the spirit world. The angels would be taken down off the wall during the night and set on the floor. No matter how many times the angels were hung back on the wall they would be discovered on the floor the next morning. Eventually they were also removed from the dining room.

It would also seem that our female spirit does not like to have her picture taken. A security camera is situated in the first-floor hallway by the stairwell. The camera caught the grainy image of the female spirit late one night. Ever since then, no such luck. Instead that same security camera has had to be replaced twice because of malfunctioning.

A number of other long-time staff members and family have contributed to the spectral stories.

Kim Smith has been employed at the Blue Elephant for ten years (as of 2012). Does she believe in spirits? Absolutely.

According to Kim, "Things have happened to me at home and at work. I often know of a conversation with another person before it takes place."

So what has Kim seen or heard during her years at the Blue Elephant?

The new brewery room is situated about three steps from the doorway to the dining room on the first floor. Here Kim has had many experiences.

"I always see a large, tall man. I can't see his face. He has a wide-brimmed hat on his head. He is wearing a long dark jacket. He is heavy set and takes up the whole frame of the doorway. I see him frequently, at least once a week or more. I can feel him looking at me."

Kim has also witnessed something else quite unusual in the building.

"In the ladies room, situated on the second floor, there are three sinks. The sink taps turn on all by themselves."

The ladies washroom where the taps turn on by themselves.

Two elderly women got the surprise of their lives one Christmas recently, when they entered the ladies room and witnessed the taps turn on and the water begin to run into the sinks as they stood there.

Kim has also seen a white misty form passing by her on the second floor.

Sarah Bertling has worked at the dining establishment for over eleven years. Today she is the chef of the Blue Elephant.

In the fall of 2001 the walk-in fridge for the kitchen was located in the basement under the original building, an old, steep staircase with very narrow stairs, led to the basement and to the kitchen fridge, and Sarah would often have to retrieve supplies from that fridge. On one occasion Sarah realized she was not alone!

"I was going down the stairs and just as I was on the fifth step I suddenly saw a pair of work boots disappear towards the cooler. That was all I could see because of the ceiling overhang above the staircase. They were old-fashioned boots and I said to myself, 'Did I just see that?'

"I knew there were no other employees down here. I wasn't scared because I believe in spirits. It is good they're here because it is some reassurance that there is something after death!"

She continued to descend the stairs.

"When I reached the basement there was no sign of anyone. The walk-in fridge door was still closed. I opened the fridge door, walked into the cooler and picked up what I needed. This happened right after the new kitchen was completed. I think we might have stirred something up."

Voices can also be heard in the building when the restaurant is closed. This happened to Sarah and a co-worker one afternoon prior to opening at 4:00 p.m.

"It was about 2:00 p.m. We didn't open that day until 4:00 p.m. Tammy a co-worker, and myself were out on the outdoor patio with Heather. Heather went to lock the front door of the building. We went back to the kitchen to continue working. I was facing the back of the kitchen and Tammy was facing the opposite direction. We were the only ones in the kitchen but we heard someone walking through the kitchen, someone we couldn't see. Then we heard an old woman's voice say 'hello'. The voice sounded like someone in their seventies.

"We looked at each other, but there was no one there. I checked the whole building. We were all alone."

Strange cutlery arrangements not done by staff.

"At one time there had been a television in the kitchen. The night staff always turned the television off. One morning the kitchen staff found the television already on. It still remains a mystery.

"When you climb up the service stairs to the second-floor hallway, there is a mirror on the wall at the far end of the hall. When you look down the hallway you can often catch a glimpse of a shadow in the mirror."

A very strange thing happened to Sarah's sister when she was working at the restaurant.

Sarah explained, "The dining room is not open until 5:00 p.m. My sister had worked in the dining room the night before. At the end of the evening she re-set the tables with clean plates and silverware before leaving for the night.

"The next day, an employee entered the dining room and observed that at one table the knife and fork were resting crossed on the napkin and the side place was set on the floor with a spoon beside it!"

Patti, another long-term employee of fourteen years, made a bizarre discovery about six years ago, while cleaning the fireplace in the dining room. The fireplace was being converted to accommodate natural gas and Patti was removing insulation from the chimney when she touched something strange.

The fireplace where the packages of candy were hidden.

"First I had touched a package of crackers and then more. Next were twenty- to twenty-five packages of unopened candy."

One would think if it had been an animal doing that there would have been evidence of eating the products. Not one package was open! The candy came from the bar area; the crackers came from the kitchen.

Pilar, the daughter of restaurant owner Heather Pond, is convinced that the Blue Elephant is haunted. She and her sister spent much of their early childhood hanging out in the attic playroom, on the third floor of the building, while their mother was working. The attic was an "eerie" place! The girls often reported hearing voices and other strange occurrences.

"We would hear someone or something shuffling around in the storage area in the attic. Lights would flicker off and on. The temperature would change suddenly and drastically from warm to cold. Not the entire attic room, but [it would change] in certain areas."

At fourteen, Pilar got the surprise of her life.

"I was walking up the stairs to the second-floor hallway when I saw something out of the corner of my eye. It was a lady wearing a blue pioneer dress. It was a long flowing dress she had on. I turned to have a closer look as she turned the corner but she had vanished. The building often freaked me out as a child. My mother never really told me about the ghost. I want to see her [the ghost], but I don't want to see her."

Pilar recalls Sundays at the Blue Elephant.

"Things would fall on Sunday, maybe an object on a shelf or counter. The coffeemaker in the pub is a good example. On two different occasions the glass coffee pot was actually picked up and dropped, shattering on the floor in the pub.

"One time I was in the office located by the kitchen on the first floor. I could hear the female ghost walking back and forth in the hallway just outside the office. The footsteps could be heard but no one was visible to the human eye."

She talked about the kitchen.

"There were jugs of oil situated on a trolley cart. Someone had taken one jug of oil and poured the oil on the floor."

Pilar heard the female presence speak. "She says hello and asks how you are doing without being seen."

She hasn't seen the male ghost but she would like to know who his is.

In 2002, a young man by the name of Tom worked at the restaurant. One day his mother came to pick him up. As a young girl she had come here for piano lessons with Gladys Borholom. In those days Gladys taught music in her studio on the second floor. While the mother waited for her son to finish work she was shocked to hear piano music coming from the second floor!

Did Gladys decide to make herself known to a former student, or did Tom's mother momentarily step back in time?

The Blue Elephant, it would seem, has many spirits present, many mysteries, some perhaps more obvious. There seems to be a strong connection to 1915 and maybe 1960 — but who is the man and who was the hoarder? Are they all connected, or are we looking at a dimensional doorway?

If you come to dine you just might see them and know for yourself.

The Black Dog
~ Lake Erie and Lake Ontario ~

*A howling dog at night means bad luck or somebody close to you
will be very sick or worse.*

FOR A CENTURY OR MORE, SAILORS HAVE FEARED THE SIGHTING OF A
Black Dog onboard ship. This canine phantom appears on vessels des-
tined for disaster. Silently, the Black Dog manifests, crosses the deck and
leaps back into the waters. No sound of a splash, but the mere sighting
of the Black Dog has caused sailors to jump ship ... they know the vessel
is doomed.

They have been forewarned!

The story of the Black Dog has its origin in the waters of the Welland
Canal in Ontario. There was a ship with a very large Newfoundland dog
for a mascot. Somehow it went overboard into the canal. According to
legend, the crew onboard showed little concern for their mascot's misfortune. Instead they made cruel sport of the dog that was swimming
for the ship. The dog was crushed to death in the gate of a canal lock.
The sound of baying remained to haunt the crew by night.

One sighting claimed the dog had eyes like coals of fire. The dog simply appears onboard a doomed ship, crosses the deck and leaps back into the water without a sound.

The *Isaac G. Jenkins*, a white, American fore-and-after ship employed in the grain trade between Chicago, Illinois and Kingston, Ontario in the 1870s, experienced the curse of the Black Dog. C.H. J. Snider wrote an article entitled "Moonlight on the Lake," an account of the curse of the Black Dog and the *Isaac G. Jenkins* schooner.

"The *Isaac G. Jenkins* was sailing down Lake Erie on a quiet night with a full moon, just enough breeze to keep her sails even. It was in the middle watch, and as peaceful as only the lakes can be on a still night. The mate and lookout were conscientiously improving the shining hour by sleeping in separate patches of shadow, carefully sheltered from the moon. The helmsman, the only man awake in the ship, was humming a broken tune from a Chicago dance hall. Suddenly he let a yell out of him which brought the mate and the lookout back from dreamland with a jerk and turned out the watch below as though the *Jenkins* were on her beam's ends in a squall. In a moment the helmsman was surrounded by half a dozen excited sailors all asking; 'What is it?' 'What is it?'

"'The Black Dog!' he gibbered. 'The Black Dog — it came up over the weather rail [safety railing] in the moonlight, all black and bristling and not a hair of it wet, and it walked across the deck and over the lee rail and into the lake without a splash.'"

The memory of that eventful night stayed with the helmsman. Later, in a Chicago bar, the helmsman was surrounded by Canadian sailors listening to his account of the Black Dog that crossed the *Isaac G. Jenkins* deck with a lolling tongue and eyes of fire, and disappeared without a trace.

The helmsman returned to the vessel and tearfully besought all hands to leave the ship and save themselves from the wrath to come.

Snider added, "The captain bestowed a kick, which lifted the helmsman on the dock. He hurled his dunnage bag after him and told him not to dare show his face again."

At Port Robinson the poor seaman appeared again and begged the captain and all hands to tie the schooner up and abandon the voyage and so to save their lives.

"He was driven off with a volley of blasphemy. But at every stopping place, as the *Isaac G. Jenkins* slowly stepped down to Lake Ontario — there were twenty-six rungs in the ladder then, and as horses towed the vessel from lock to lock, he would bob up and wail his warning.

"His last appearance occurred when the two horses were being unhitched after she had been dragged across the pond above Muir's drydock, at Port Dalhousie," stated Snider.

The captain, fearing his crew would mutiny, quickly set sail. It was November of 1875. As evening drew near it blew hard from the southwest, a fair wind for Oswego and home for the *Isaac G. Jenkins*.

Snider described that night. "At the end of a fortnight of westerly gales, seventy-five sailing vessels lay in Kingston Harbour, grain laden from the upper lakes, and, of course, the crews visited, and every forecastle was filled with the story of the Black Dog."

John S. Parsons, a well-known ship chandler, recalled a few years later that many Oswego schooners were in Port Dalhousie when the *Isaac G. Jenkins* hurried out to her fate.

Snider added, "The *Nevada*, almost a duplicate of the *Jenkins*, and the *Sam Cook*, got into Oswego next morning by the skin of their teeth, for the wind had gone from south-west to north-west and blew a living gale. It raised an appalling sea down in the Oswego corner of the lake."

The brigantine *Montcalm* struggled to make Oswego and made a run down the lake and into the St. Lawrence River. The captain did later report that he had been in company with the *Isaac G. Jenkins* as far as Thirty Mile Point, but lost sight of her when the gale struck.

The *Isaac G. Jenkins* never made it home. Snider explained, "They watched and waited for her and other Oswego vessels. They sent tugs up the lake when the gale abated. The tugs went all the way to Port Dalhousie, and there found the rest of the fleet, wind bound. The breeze had fallen light and ahead after the gale, and the other schooners waited for weather. Some were towed home by the Oswego tugs, some sailed down, but not the *Jenkins*."

There was however, one survivor of the *Isaac G. Jenkins*. A short time later a farmer sighted a dog coming ashore at Sheldon's Pond some miles up the westward of Oswego. The farmer noted, "He was a strange dog and he seemed all in. His hair stuck to his sides as if glued there, and he dragged his hind legs as though paralyzed."

The dog was later brought to town and recognized as Captain John Brown's dog from the *Jenkins*.

The seven crewmembers of the *Issac G. Jenkins* had simply vanished.

On November 19, 1881, the Black Dog warned another ship, the *Mary Jane*. On that fateful day the *Mary Jane* was carrying a load of telephone poles when a storm drove it ashore, causing it to smash to pieces near Port Rowan, Ontario. All nine crewmembers were lost.

Dock workers on the wharves at Port Colborne later reported that prior to the *Mary Jane* sailing on its final journey they had witnessed a Black Dog leaping from the schooner and vanishing upon setting foot on the dock.

According to a book entitled *Ghosts and Spirits* by Chambers Harrap Publishers Ltd., "Large black spectral dogs are said to haunt places such as crossroads and churchyards; legends of Black Dogs are common all over the British Isles, with each area calling the apparition by a different name.

"Black Dogs have a number of characteristics that set them apart from the phantoms of [other] domestic dogs. These include their great size [they are frequently described as being as big as a calf] and their eyes, which are large and luminous, often described as blazing red saucers."

The Black Dog is described as walking through solid objects and its appearance is frequently said to be accompanied by lightning or fire or an explosion. It is usually seen at night. It leaves no tracks, and makes no sound as it walks.

Black Dogs have supposedly left physical traces in the form of burns or scratches on places or people.

Chambers adds, "The appearance of a Black Dog is often interpreted as an omen of impending death or disaster for the person witnessing it.

"A study conducted in the 1970s by Ivan Burns suggested that Black Dogs have an affinity for bodies of water such as rivers, streams, and the sea."

The sighting of a phantom prior to a disaster is not uncommon. Such spectres are not responsible for a tragedy, but rather are a warning in order to prevent the loss of life. The Grey Man of Pawleys Island, South Carolina is just such an apparition. His appearance foretells a hurricane.

Originally, Pawleys Island was inhabited by the Waccamaw and Winah Indians. One of the first European settlers was George Pawley, a wealthy rice plantation owner. In the 1800s several plantation families took up residence on the island in an effort to escape the extreme heat and malaria-carrying mosquitoes on the mainland.

There are several variations of the tale of the Grey Man. My favourite story is this one told by Professor Alan Brown.

"A young girl whose father owned a house on Pawleys Island was engaged to a young man who had gone to fight with General Washington in the Revolutionary War. After several months, the young man returned to Georgetown by ship. After disembarking, he was so eager to see the girl on Pawleys Island that he took a hazardous route across the marsh instead of using one of the causeways. He had not ridden very far before his horse became mired in mud. His servant watched helplessly as the young man sank out of sight."

A short time after his funeral the young girl was strolling along the beach, when a strange greyish-coloured figure that resembled her fiancé appeared before her. In a trembling voice, he said, "Leave before a hurricane destroys the island." He then vanished.

Terrified, she ran home and informed her father of what happened. The father made the decision to leave immediately with his family. Later that same day a hurricane pummelled Pawleys Island, destroying many of the homes there.

The Grey Man has been sighted here for many generations. He was seen in 1822, 1893, 1916, 1954, 1955, and 1995, just before a hurricane struck the island.

I, myself, have met more than one person who has encountered the Grey Man.

Another warning of doom that was told of on Lake Huron was the playing of the violin. The only account I have heard of personally was also a ship's mate. When he told his mother he dreamed of a violin playing, she told him not to board the ship. Although he warned the crew he did not go aboard and the ship, indeed, went down.

So, if the Black Dog or the Grey Man appears before you or a violin should play upon your dreams, take heed. Be forewarned and avoid disaster.

The Baldoon Mystery

~ Baldoon, Ontario ~

(no longer exists — formerly situated near Wallaceburg, Ontario)

TO TANGLE WITH A WITCH CAN OFTEN LEAD TO MISERY AND DISASTER. The Baldoon Mysteries is such a tale taken place over one hundred and seventy years ago in rural Ontario.

Our story begins with John McDonald and his family, who experienced several spine-tingling events at the Baldoon Settlement. Nervous of future occurrences and the possibility that their lives were in danger, the McDonalds struggled against invisible dark forces. They were plagued by some malevolent energy that interrupted their lives and defied explanation. Nothing seemed to function as it should. Surely, they had been cursed.

What was Baldoon really like? The community was located in southwestern Ontario, on low, wet lands that were surveyed in 1802. It was Lord Alexander Selkirk who sought to attract Scottish Highlanders to the area. In return for this, Selkirk himself would be granted one hundred and fifty acres free for every colonist he procured. It would seem that the settlement of Baldoon was founded on less-than-benevolent principles. These early colonists had no way of knowing just how uninhabitable this land really was. By 1804, however, the first settlers' eager anticipation had vanished into the mist.

Despite difficult circumstances, the newcomers laboured to create a new life here. One determined soul was the aforementioned John McDonald. Around 1804 he and his wife built a sturdy frame house in Baldoon. For a short time John and his beloved lived in peace and soon heard the *pit-a-pat* of little feet. It was, however, a short-lived dream. A series of mysterious persecutions began to plague the McDonalds. John and his family did not live in isolation; a very unusual family resided close by. Others in the area referred to this family as "the people of the long, low, log house"; they were a family that consisted of an old woman, her two sons, and one daughter. They were somewhat reclusive and unsociable people, with few associations in their community.

The land of John McDonald had long been coveted by the people of the long, low, log house. They approached him on several occasions with offers of purchase, but John always refused. (Was this decision connected to all the mysteries he and his family encountered?)

In those days, wives wove homespun cloth for clothing and straw into hats for protection from the blazing sun. These were shared activities among the settlers. One fine day, while the men were occupied with farm duties, the young women gathered at the McDonald barn to pick and prepare straw for an afternoon of hat-making. The barn was built of logs and inside it there were poles that stretched from side to side overhead, forming hangers for the flax.

As the women sat chatting and working they were startled when one of the flax-laden poles came loose and plummeted to the floor. Although the pole fell right in their midst, it struck no one. Then a second of these poles crashed, and a third! The ladies fled to the house. No sooner were they inside then there was the crash of glass — and a lead bullet lay at their feet. Another bullet shattered the window, and another, until finally, a shower of bullets came and the young women fled the house. There were no explanations for this.

For a few days, all was peaceful on the McDonald farm. Then, one evening, close to midnight, John was awakened by the sound of marching men, moving backwards and forwards with measured steps, then stillness, then more heavy tramping. Although he searched for the source of the sound, no one was to be seen. For three successive years, many unexplainable manifestations afflicted the McDonald family.

Bullets through the windows became a daily occurrence. John finally barricaded the windows with heavy boards. The bullets came through the wood, without a mark! By this time the whole countryside was aware, alert, and alarmed.

John McDonald was really beside himself. He and his family were anxious and tense from this relentless activity. They had been haunted by noises in the night; cups and saucers regularly flew through the air, and even their house was reported to literally rise at one end or the other as much as one metre (three feet).

An officer in the British army, Captain Lewis Bennett, visited Baldoon specifically to meet with the McDonald family and to examine the situation. During his visit his own gun exploded for no apparent reason. Bennett witnessed the haunting first-hand. One incident involved a baby in a cradle who suddenly began to scream as though in pain. She could not be consoled but, when picked up, a hot stone was discovered beneath the blankets. When the stone was removed another appeared. This was repeated several times. Little balls of fire were seen floating in mid-air and settling in various parts of the house. Every room in the house experienced this kind of fire.

The haunting began to intensify. McDonald was exhausted and desperate. The family was not safe. Then one day flames burst out in a dozen places simultaneously and, although the family escaped, the house and its contents were lost to the flames.

John and his family moved to the safety of his father's house and life seemed to return to normal. But it was not over. Once more the fearful tramping started, day and night; the furniture moved about and a heavy kitchen cupboard fell to the floor with a thud. McDonald sought help, this time from one Reverend McDorman. He was different, at least for a man of the cloth — he acknowledged the dark side. McDorman told McDonald that he knew of a Doctor Troyer, and his daughter; both had the gift of second sight and the mystical power to do stone readings.

Dr. Troyer was a competent botanist and quite familiar about the medicinal properties of the flora and his forest home.

The doctor was known to be quite superstitious. Harry Barrett, in his book entitled *Lore and Legends of Long Point*, describes Dr. Troyer. "He seemed to possess extra-sensory perception or 'second sight.' Because of his other gifts and superstitions he became known as the witch doctor!"

At the time, Dr. Troyer was suffering quite badly. He had been hexed sometime before by witches. Barrett explains, "Troyer attributed all his mental and physical aches and pains to the evil spells the ladies of the night had cast over him. As he grew older, his terror of them grew — to the point where he bolted a large bear trap [witch trap] to the floor at the foot of his bed and set it nightly to deter the witches."

However, Dr. Troyer still believed they periodically took him from his home in the middle of the night. Barrett adds, "In spite of such precautions, he believed the witches periodically removed him from his home, transformed him into a domestic animal, and forced the poor creature to take part in their evil activities. He often related how he had been snatched from a peaceful sleep, turned into a horse, and ridden by his tormentors across Lake Erie to Dunkirk, where they attended a clandestine dance."

Following this hair raising experience Dr Troyer followed a long, involved treatment of herbs to help regain his health.

Dr. Troyer's witch trap

The doctor and daughter would spend time practicing their gift of clairvoyance by staring, in a trance-like state, into a large moonstone. They believed that by doing this, they could see the location of articles neighbours believed to be lost or stolen.

John McDonald implored the reverend to take him to see Dr. Troyer. Together they travelled for several days to reach Long Point, on the shore of Lake Erie, where the girl and her father lived.

John told the young girl of the many mysterious happenings.

She listened intently and asked, "Did you ever have any trouble about a piece of land?"

"Not exactly trouble," replied John.

"Did one of your neighbours desire to purchase a portion of your land and did you refuse?" asked the girl.

McDonald nodded.

The girl replied, "People in a long, low, log house?"

McDonald said, "Yes."

Turning to her stone, the girl remained in a trance-like state for some time. Eventually, she asked, "Have you seen a stray black goose in your flock?"

The log cabin at Long Point where Dr. Troyer lived.

"Yes," he replied.

She continued, "In that bird lives the destroyer of your peace. It has taken the shape of a bird and it is your enemy. You shall mould a bullet of sterling silver and fire it at the bird. If you wound it, your enemy shall be wounded in some corresponding part of their body. Go and be at peace."

Upon his return, McDonald did as the young girl said. He and a party of men located a flock of geese by the river. He drew a bead on the black goose in the flock. The strange bird cried out like a human when it was wounded and made its way to the reeds with a broken wing.

Determinedly, John turned his footsteps toward the marsh, where the long, low, log house stood. One anxious look revealed all. There sat the old woman resting in a chair – and she had a broken arm. When she saw him, she pulled back.

For John McDonald and his family, no spiritual manifestations were ever seen or heard of again. Fact, it would seem, is truly stranger than fiction.

Stealing the Dead

~ St. Thomas, Ontario ~

*Light twelve candles around a corpse to protect the soul of the
deceased from evil forces; ghosts and demons cannot cross
into a circle of lighted candles.*

SOME PEOPLE BELIEVE THE SOUL LEAVES THE BODY AT THE PRECISE TIME
of death. The soul then remains near the body for up to three days or
longer before leaving this physical plane. But why would that be true?

Many traditions say the soul has three days to say goodbye to
the living. Perhaps it is also there to guard the body until it has been
appropriately honoured. After all, the deceased body may in some
cases haunt the living! The butcher's wife is such an example.

Our story begins in 1849. Samuel Paddon and his family were poor
farmers, living in the rural region of Marhamchurh, Cornwall County,
England. The family grew what they could and yet barely survived. A
brother-in-law who had left England and settled in the south western
district of what is now Ontario, Canada, wrote to the Paddon family to
share his experiences. This encouraged Samuel to think about emigrating

and getting a fresh start in life. However, there was a problem — money. Samuel didn't have any money and could only borrow enough to make the journey alone. It was decided he should go and send for his wife Mary, and his daughter Ann, at a later date.

Samuel followed his brother-in-law to St. Thomas, Ontario. Once there he established himself as a butcher. Two years later he was able to acquire a property on present-day Lynhurst Hills. He built a house and then he sent for his wife and daughter.

According to a direct descendant, Susan Paddon in an article she wrote entitled, "Something about a Butcher's wife," she stated, "In the spring of 1852, Mary and Ann did finally arrive, and immediately fell in love with their new home and the fresh start they were about to make.

"But, as every happy occurrence seems to have a sad one to follow, Samuel's wife, Mary, became dreadfully ill in the fall of 1857, and shortly thereafter, on December 3, died of consumption."

Mary Paddon's funeral was held on January 1, 1858, at the Old English Church and her body was buried in the adjoining cemetery.

Poor Samuel was beside himself. One would think he would adjust and carry on with his life and attend to his surviving daughter, Ann, but that was not the case. Mary, Samuel's deceased wife, rose from the grave, shortly after her death. She didn't rise up alone, she had some help!

Two spirits make an appearance in the St. Thomas cemetery. The second spirit can be seen just behind the head of the first spirit.

Susan Paddon described what happened. "On January 12, 1858, a grave keeper was making his routine rounds of the yard at the St. Thomas Church when he happened to notice something strange about one of the graves. It was Mary's grave. The surrounding earth had been freshly turned."

The next day the grave keeper, along with several other men. investigated Mary's gravesite. They found that the corpse had been removed from the casket; however, Mary's grave clothes had been removed from her body and were left at the gravesite.

The people of St. Thomas were alarmed at the discovery and concerned about their loved ones below the ground. Questions arose. What had happened to Mary? Where did she go? Could the dead rise up, and walk again? Had someone stolen the body?

After two days of searching St. Thomas, Mary's body was found. That is, was left of her. She had been hidden in the Odd Fellow's Lodge. The Metcalfe Building housed both the Odd Fellow's Lodge and the Orangemen's Hall. There was a coroner's inquest concerning Mary Paddon and it told the tale of this heinous crime. What it did not reveal was how the discovery of Mary's body haunted her husband, Samuel, for the rest of his life.

The following is the evidence sworn before Elijah E. Duncombe, M.D., coroner for the County of Elgin, on Monday the 18th day of January, 1858.

On that day, the jury were sworn in and they chose Dr. H. Wade as their foreman.

Susan's father, Dean Paddon, stated, "My daughter Susan Paddon introduced this ghastly event to readers in the first issue of *Memories of St. Thomas and Elgin*, in her story, 'Something About a Butcher's Wife.' This was based on information passed down from my father, Russ Paddon, to me, then from me to Susan."

"John Paddon, (Samuel's father) Sworn, saith that the body now in the room was the wife of his son; she died on the 30th of December 1857, and was buried in the cemetery near this town, on the 1st January 1858.

"I first mistrusted that the body was missing from the grave. After examining the grave, I found the body was removed, but none of the grave clothes. I searched houses, but could not find the body. I am certain that is the body [before him] of my son's wife. I was not present when it was found; I knew it by one of the toes being turned under the other. I mentioned this circumstance to several persons before I saw the body.

"Samuel Paddon, (husband) Sworn, saith I have examined the body now in the room, and recognized it as that of my wife; I corroborate my father's evidence as to the time of her decease and am well satisfied it is her body by the hair and the hand; I was present when the body was found. I first suspected the body was in this building; I had been informed that Dr. Caughill had been implicated in raising a body sometime since. I went to him and asked leave to search his surgery; he hesitated and asked me my reason, and I said, that as he had been implicated in raising up of Mrs. Anderson, some time since. Then Mr. Sparling came in and said that it was likely the students Maitland, Mann, Miller, Fizsimons, and others, who had gone to Toronto some days after my wife was buried had taken the body with them, for he said it must have been taken the second or third night after the funeral, or it would be decomposed.

"I was told next day Saturday, that Sparling said he would give twenty dollars for a dead body, hard as times were, and also that he was studying medicine under Dr. Caughill."

Samuel revealed another clue to his predicament when Sparling arrived at his stall in the market and inquired if Samuel had seen any trace of his wife yet. Samuel, "I said I have not, although I have impressions on my mind that I cannot erase. Sparling responded, 'Oh you will never find it [Mary], those young men that have gone to Toronto have taken it with them.' I said they could not, as the grave had not been disturbed until after they were gone. He then said it may have been taken to Fingal, or perhaps Boston or New York. He said 'In this weather a body would keep easier for five months rather than one month in warm weather.'"

Samuel became more suspicious of Sparling because he knew something about the body. He concluded that his wife's body was in the Metcalfe Building where the Orangemen's Lodge and Odd Fellows rented space for their practices and meetings.

Samuel obtained a warrant to search the Metcalfe Building.

"We arrived at the building but none of the Dr.s [sic] were present. We came up to the third storey, tried to open several doors that were locked, but could not find the keys. I heard that Sparling was the head of one of the lodges and was told that he might have the keys. I then went to Mr. Drake to find out if there was any part of the building let besides what the Orangemen and Odd Fellows had. He said 'Yes, Sparling has rented one and got the key about a week ago."

Samuel then requested Mr. Drake to come along with him. If he could not get the key, Samuel was going to break open the door. Drake still did not wish to join Samuel. In the meantime, Constable Campbell and Mr. King informed Samuel that they had seen inside Sparling's room and saw blood and flesh on the floor, as if a body had lain there.

Samuel then found Sparling in Dr. Caughill's surgery.

"I asked Sparling if he knew who had a key to the Orangemen's Lodge; he said he did not know and that he never had it in his life. I said 'I had heard you were the head of the lodge and you must know who keeps the key.' He said that there were two lodges, James Drake was master of one, and he was the other, but he did not know who had the key."

Realizing the body of Mary Paddon had been removed from Sparling's rented room, Samuel, along with Campbell, arrived at the doorway of a room used as the Orange Hall, in the upper storey of the Metcalfe buildings.

"We then broke open the door and Campbell said 'here is the body,' — that it was in a bag, all but the intestines, they were scattered about, the brain was in a tin can by itself. They cut open the bag, and at once recognized the body as that of my late wife."

Dr. C. Hall later stated at the inquest, "I have examined the body and have no doubt that the cutting on the body has been for the purpose of dissection."

Benjamin Drake shed some incredible light on the situation. He acknowledged that he had rented a room to Sparling for a year for the purpose of him studying medicine.

Sparling had notified Drake that he indeed brought the body there, and had taken it from the burying ground. I also recalled him saying 'we' concerning the taking of the body. Drake then cautioned Sparling to not tell him too much, he did not want to know.

When Dr. Caughill was asked about the body, he revealed that he was aware that there was a body in Sparling's room, but never knew it to be there before that night of discovery. Dr. Sanderson stated he had no hand in bringing the body to the building.

The jury, after hearing the testimony, returned a verdict: "That the body is fully proven to be the body of the late Mrs. Samuel Paddon. That the jury find by indispensable evidence, that the body so found, was taken out the graveyard known as the St. Thomas Cemetery, and that such body was taken out of the ground by William F. Sparling, shoe-maker of this town and by others to the jurors unknown.

"That the jurors have great reason to complain of the unsatisfactory answers given by Dr. Caughill, W. F. Sparling, and Dr. Sanderson to questions which, in the opinion of the jury were calculated to bring out facts necessary to the investigation and have to express their disapprobation of the same; as also the abhorrence in which they hold the sacrilegious removal of the sacred dead and would strongly urge that all legal means should be used to bring the guilty parties to justice."

At the end of January, the adjourned examination of W.F. Sparling and Dr. Caughill, for their participation in the mutilation of the body of Mary Paddon, took place at the courthouse. Sparling never showed up and Dr. Caughill was bound over for a later date. The court received information that Sparling had gone to Detroit where he was likely to remain. He chose to stay there rather than going to jail here.

For Samuel Paddon, this horrendous experience had lasting consequences. According to Susan Paddon, "Samuel met another young woman by the name of Dinah Oliver, whom he later married and with whom he had seven children.

"A man of Christian beliefs, Samuel had lost his trust in humanity and could never reconcile his own mortality.

"Although Samuel lived to be an old man he suffered tremendously from chronic nightmares in which he would see himself buried alive, only to be exhumed and cut open by the robbers of his own dear, sweet Mary's grave."

As for his new wife, Samuel needed to check her vital signs nine to ten times a day to reassure himself that her health was good.

The grave robbing of Mary Paddon and the dissection of the woman haunted Samuel to his grave. One would hope that his death in 1886, at the age of eighty-one years, released his soul from the agony of his lifetime. Who knows, he may still be here in spirit guarding his resting place.

As for W.F. Sparling, he became a surgeon in the Union army during the Civil War in the United States.

Eldon House

~ London, Ontario ~

There will be death soon if:
There is a knock on the wall near the bed of an invalid
You dream of a black candle
A clock which has not been working suddenly chimes
A mirror falls and breaks by itself
A black beetle runs over your shoes

COMMITMENT IS SUCH A POWERFUL AND BINDING FORCE THAT ON occasion can reach beyond the living and manifest in the world of the dead. Such was the case of Lieutenant Wynniatte of the British garrison of London, Ontario who promised to honour the request of Sarah Harris to attend the ball at Eldon House on May 14, 1841.

The story of Eldon House begins with John Harris born in Devon, England in 1782. Harris served in the merchant marines prior to 1803, when he was impressed (ordered) into the Royal Navy. He eventually rose to the rank of Master which, while not an officer's rank was a key position on board a ship. His responsibilities included maintaining, outfitting and navigating the ship. He also noted and described features of coastlines that had yet to be recorded on charts.

During the War of 1812 he accompanied Sir James Lucas Yeo to North America to fight the Americans on the Great Lakes.

Following the end of the War of 1812, he was ordered to assist with a survey of the Great Lakes under Commodore Edward Owen. One of his first assignments was to survey the north shore of Lake Erie for a shipbuilding site.

Arriving at Port Ryerse, on Lake Erie on April 10, 1815, he met a seventeen-year-old woman by the name of Amelia, the daughter of the ports founder, Samuel Ryerse, a United Empire Loyalist.

John and Amelia fell in love and married on June 28, 1815. The couple took up residence in Kingston, Ontario until 1817, when John retired on half-pay from the navy.

By 1821 John and Amelia relocated to a farm near Long Point in Woodhouse Township. That same year John was appointed Treasurer of the London District. His job entailed tax collecting as well as bridge construction. The District Courthouse was located a short distance away in Vittora until 1825, when the courthouse was moved to London, Ontario.

In 1834 John began the construction of Eldon House, situated on a piece of high ground overlooking the forks of the Thames River and near the District Courthouse in London.

The house was a two-storey Georgian style structure with a hip roof and a centre hall plan. A small portico ornamented the main entrance until the 1870s, when it was replaced with a sweeping verandah.

John and Amelia settled into their home with their eight children. Eventually two more children would be born, bringing the number to seven girls and three boys in total.

In the early years the estate was named Eldon Terrace, since a number of terraces had been created down the side of the bank to provide a picturesque view and a pleasant walk to the river.

Located on the flats of the river was an enormous vegetable garden where corn, potatoes, carrots, and some three thousand roots of celery were grown.

In its heyday Eldon House employed a staff of five men to manage the maintenance of the grounds, greenhouse, nursery plot, flower and vegetable gardens. The staff was reduced to three men in the winter.

The first recorded sighting of a spirit occurred on May 14, 1841. The haunting revolves around commitment and untimely death and a hall clock.

Family diaries record many social activities at Eldon House, especially visits by young officers of the British regiments stationed at London between 1839 and 1852. It was during one of these festive events at Eldon House that death came knocking and passed through the hallway to join the ball.

Twenty-six-year-old Lieutenant Wynniatt of the British garrison, a young suitor of Sarah Harris had promised to attend the ball to be held at Eldon Terrance on May 14, 1841.

The afternoon before the ball, the lieutenant decided to take a ride on horseback. At some point he was seen up the River Thames towards a Mr. Jennings sawmill. Before leaving his residence, Lieutenant Wynniatt had asked his male servant to have his evening clothes laid out saying he intended to go out to the party at Eldon Terrace and might be late coming home.

When the evening arrived and the lieutenant failed to appear at the ball, Sarah was quite disappointed. Despite this she joined in the dancing being held in the largest room of the house situated to the right of the hallway near the front entrance.

While dancing, Sarah became quite excited when she caught a glimpse of Lieutenant Wynniatt standing in the hallway at the entrance-way of the room.

There he stood looking calmly and steadily at her. Then Sarah became alarmed that he did not enter the room to speak to her.

In 1897 W. T. Stead, author of *Real Ghost Stories*, wrote an account of this event.

"The lieutenant was also noticed by Sarah's father, John Harris, and her sister, who both spoke to him and were surprised and hurt, when, without a word he turned away. He continued walking down the hallway.

"In the meantime Sarah Harris followed him down the hallway and happened to glance at the hall clock and noted the time — 6:00 p.m. The lieutenant then turned left towards the back kitchen area and vanished from sight."

Sarah, her father, and her sister thought the entire incident was quite bizarre and without explanation.

The next morning Lieutenant Wynniatt's servant arrived at Eldon Terrace to enquire after his master's whereabouts. The lieutenant had not returned home that night. Yet, his horse and dog had arrived at a neighbourhood farmhouse!

William E. Hutchins, in an article entitled "In Search of the Ghost of Eldon House," wrote, "Suspicions got afloat that all was not right and a diligent search was immediately set on foot for the body. Although the whole garrison and many hundred civilians were almost in hourly search, no trace of the body was discovered."

Subsequently it was discovered that the saddle the lieutenant had been using was wet, and therefore a search was conducted along the River Thames till night without success.

On the morning of Sunday, May 16, 1841, a party of searchers, accompanied by some Aboriginal guides, discovered the body. The unfortunate officer lay embedded in sand in the middle of the river in deep water.

The coroner, Dr. Moore, deduced that in attempting to ford the River Thames, the deceased was either thrown or had fallen from his horse and had drowned.

There was a startling discovery made at the scene of the accident. Lieutenant Wynniatt's pocket watch he had been wearing had stopped at precisely 6:00 p.m. The same time he had been seen walking by the hall clock at Eldon Terrace.

The good lieutenant had kept his promise to his loved one. He did indeed attend the festivities as promised, even in death.

Some people believe that he still appears at Eldon House on May 14th each year at 6:00 p.m. to see the lovely Sarah Harris. However, our story doesn't end here.

In 1850 John Harris died; Amelia remained living at Eldon House. Four daughters of Amelia had all married military officers and left home. Her eldest son John, a lawyer and in partnership with brothers Edward and George, had every intention to live at Eldon House. However, he succumbed to a lingering illness two years later. His brother Edward and his wife Sophie remained at Eldon House with Amelia.

The year 1867 revealed the very spiritual forces at work in Eldon House. Amelia was nearing her seventieth year. She commented frequently about being alone and her loss of vitality. As she put it, "We all have to journey the same road. It would not be called the dark valley if the approach to it were not gloomy."

She had endured a series of trials and tribulations. The tragic deaths of several children — Charlotte (1854), Helen (1861), and John (1861) — left her lonely and bereft of familial company. Four adult daughters lived overseas.

She was prone to bouts of depression; her diary often marked a preoccupation with death, especially in the context of her dreams.

Amelia had thought about death for many years. Dreams and the interpretation of them constituted another insight into her psyche. According to her diary, her dreams were connected with the deaths of her husband, son, and daughters. They may have remained close to her in spirit. Apparently the dreams had a profound spiritual significance for her. Amelia had a reoccurring dream of going home, which she claimed to have had for fifty years. Her dream destination was her old home at Port Ryerse. She claimed to have had over one hundred dreams during her last fifty years of life.

In one diary entry, recorded in 1861, she wrote that she had actually got home for the second time in all her dreams. This prompted her to predict that perhaps the third visit would mark her return to where "I may be home in earnest."

For her this meant the return to past happiness with loved ones. In another dream she saw the future when she would be "at rest" with the loved ones who had gone before. Amelia died in 1882 at the age of eighty-two.

It was during the 1880s that another odd event occurred at Eldon House that quite possibly led to another spirit encounter. There is no explanation as to why, but the Harris brothers received and kept the head of a murderer who had been hanged in London in August of 1830.

His name was Cornelius Burleigh. The story of Burleigh began on the morning of September 16, 1829, when a constable Pomeroy was in hot pursuit of the culprit responsible for theft, arson, and killing cattle in the area. Pomeroy was ambushed by the thief (or was it thieves?) and shot dead. One clue was found at the scene of the crime — a cap!

Officials believed the cap belonged to Cornelius Burleigh, a resident of London.

A reward of one hundred pounds was posted by the district authorities for the capture of Burleigh. In short order Burleigh was apprehended. At the time of his arrest, Cornelius Burleigh firmly expressed his innocence of any crime. During his incarceration that winter the other prisoners in the jail made a break for freedom. Cornelius, certain of his acquittal, remained behind. As a result some citizens had doubts about his guilt. Would he not, after all, have escaped along with the other prisoners if he were guilty?

Unfortunately for Burleigh, others did not agree that he was innocent, including the witnesses who testified against him. The jury found him guilty of murder. He was sentenced to be hanged until dead in August of 1830.

By Thursday, August 19, 1830, the size of the settlement of London had grown from three hundred residents to three thousand. Spectators travelled from nearby townships and from York, as Toronto was called then, and Hamilton to witness this public execution.

At the time a Reverend Jackson was on a dedicated mission to elicit a confession from Burleigh. After all, he surmised, there was no harm in it if he gained a small amount of fame and fortune doing God's work.

According to Jackson, it only took a mere forty-one hours prior to his execution to gain a dying confession. Jackson, along with Reverends. Boswell and Smith, described the ordeal stating, "Burleigh burst into a flood of tears."

In no time, the Reverend Jackson had the confession printed in handbill form to sell to the public at the cost of $1.50.

Jackson read the dying confession from the scaffold. Edward Bosell, an Anglican missionary, proceeded to baptize the twenty-six-year-old Burleigh and to give him Holy Communion.

The spectators waited in anticipation as the hangman placed the noose around his neck. But something went wrong! The rope could not bear the condemned man's weight. As Burleigh was about to swing, the rope snapped and he dropped twenty feet to the ground, dazed but alive.

"Burleigh's conversion was complete. He walked among the crowd with the tail end of the broken rope dangling from his neck. His whole mind devoted to prayer, praise, singing, and thanksgiving," according to Orlo Miller, a London historian and author.

Burleigh truly believed the God had saved him, but the authorities had something else in mind. Someone was ordered to fetch a new rope from Goodhues store across the way. They were going to hang him again!

One can only imagine Burleigh's horror when he was led back up the scaffold stairway. The second attempt was successful but it wasn't over yet.

The crowd then waited in eager anticipation to watch the public dissection of Burleigh's body by medical professionals of the District of London and their students in the open courtyard.

Surgeons at the time could only use corpses of the condemned for teaching purposes. The doctors and students quite literally cut Cornelius Burleigh to pieces.

However, a special portion of the remains had already been spoken for by a man named Orson Squire Fowler. This undergraduate from Yale University had the presence of mind to obtain Burleigh's head. Fowler, it seems, was well versed in the science of phrenology.

According to Webster's Dictionary, phrenology is "the study of the shape and size of the cranium as a supposed indication of character and mental faculties."

Prior to the hanging, Burleigh had consented to see Fowler, who examined his head and jotted down findings — although it was to no avail for Burleigh. It was not until the dissection of Burleigh's body that Fowler conducted a lecture in the dimly lit hall with the skull and a candle to illustrate the truth of his assertions. The geography of Burleigh's cranium bore out his predictions. Where he had said the skull walls were thin, the candlelight shone through, in other areas no light emerged. It was Fowler's contention that the bumps on Burleigh's skull proved conclusively that he was incapable of murder, that officials had hanged the wrong man.

For the next fifty years Fowler travelled extensively, using Burleigh's skull to promote his theory of phrenology as a method of criminal assessment. In the 1880s Fowler returned to London and, for whatever reason, gave Burleigh's skull to the Harris family, who lived at Eldon House.

The spirit of Cornelius Burleigh was reported to haunt Eldon House for years to come. Also during this time Edward Harris and Sophia were experiencing some financial problems that threatened the loss of Eldon House. Edward's brother, George and his wife Lucy sold their home and moved into Eldon House to help ease the financial burdens of the family.

In the 1890s Lucy Harris received a substantial inheritance, which greatly improved the family fortune.

Instead of marrying, Amelia (Milly) Harris, the daughter of George and Lucy, eventually chose to remain and care for Eldon House, until her death in 1952. Following her death Ronald Harris and his wife Lana who had lived at Eldon House with Milly and raised their children there donated the home, property and collections to the City of London.

In 1961 Eldon House became a public museum, highlighting the times and lives of the Harris family.

Strange as it may seem, Cornelius Burleigh's head was placed on display in the museum as a historical curiousity. The museum even sold postcards of Burleigh's head.

It's not surprising that stories of Eldon House being haunted soon began circulating in the community. Perhaps public activity in the building began to stir things up. In 2001, I wrote a book entitled *Fit to be Tied*, in which I highlighted the hanging of Cornelius Burleigh and his head being on display at Eldon House. Somehow, some distant relatives living in Michigan received a copy of the book. They immediately made arrangements to travel to London and acquire the head of Cornelius in order to give him a proper burial.

However, items of the unusual did not stop there concerning Eldon House. In fact, the house contains many strange artifacts that all have stories and may very well pertain to spirit activity of the place.

The Harris family — like many opulent families of their time and place — travelled extensively to many faraway places in the late 1800s and early 1900s. During these expeditions family members would collect remarkable items of interest to bring back home. For example, in 1897 George and Lucy Harris and their daughter, Milly, went on an eight-month trip to visit Japan, China, Burma, India, Egypt, and Palestine.

When touring Eldon House today you can occasionally sense you are not alone in the dwelling. Portraits seem to stare back at you in passing.

You can feel uncomfortable catching your own image in a hall or bedroom mirror. Is it really you that you are seeing?

The air in the house moves about as if someone or something has just gone by you. A second glance at the bedroom curtains is required to ensure they didn't move when you first entered the room.

Material artifacts or personal items have long been connected or associated with the spirit world. For example, the Adamsons of Port Credit, Ontario travelled around the world in the 1890s. Egypt was one of the most popular stops, including the need to see the Valley of the Kings. The source of haunting in the Adamson estate came from the attic. The very soul of the Adamson lineage remained shrouded in darkness. They should never have brought back the mummy's hand from ancient Egypt and placed it in the attic of the home. Once the energy had been released, the spirit activity exploded. Letters bound in trunks and diaries, not to mention locks of Victorian hair, all added to a toxic brew resulting in death.

Artifacts from far-away destinations decorate the interior of Eldon House. The artifacts that caught my eye and nudged my soul were the spears collected on the wall near the kitchen. The one spear, its handle decorated with human hair, once belonged to a head-hunter from Borneo. This item caused a severe disturbance in my energy field.

Nancy Johnson, a historical interpretor at Eldon House has worked there for the past eight years. During the first few days on the job a man entered the premise and walked straight ahead to the central staircase leading to the second floor bedrooms. He looked at Nancy and remarked, "I can't go upstairs."

Nancy replied, "That's okay. You're more than welcome to tour the downstairs."

The man answered, "You don't understand, I can't go upstairs."

Nancy remained somewhat puzzled by the comment.

Then he explained to her what he really meant.

"I have visited Eldon House on two separate occasions. Each time I went upstairs and as I reached halfway up the stairs someone started tugging at my pant leg."

He indicated to Nancy exactly where on the staircase this had happened to him.

Nancy politely acknowledged his comments.

To be honest Nancy told me she would indeed like to see a spirit, but to date has never encountered one.

On another occasion a woman and her children arrived to tour Eldon House. According to Nancy, "One of the children suddenly blurted out, 'my mother is psychic.'"

Nancy decided to share the story of the man's experience on the staircase with the mother. She pointed out that she never told the woman where on the staircase this even had happened. Nancy shared what occurred next.

"The woman began to climb the staircase and then stopped exactly where the man had the paranormal experience."

Nancy added, "She said she felt a coldness in the area."

The woman continued, "I feel the presence of a woman here. She is happy with what you're doing here at Eldon House."

Visitors also experience spirits on the second floor of the building where the bedrooms are located. The wife of a doctor attending a conference in London approached Nancy after touring the house. The woman only had one question for Nancy. "Have you seen the face in the mirror in the Green Room?"

The Green Room was the bedroom of Edward and Sophie Harris.

Eldon House is a remarkable structure to visit. It is a timeless keepsake of love, commitment, and undying devotion. It is a place visited by the living yet still occupied by the spirits of the past.

Greystones Inn

~ Orangeville, Ontario ~

If thirteen people sit down at a table to eat, one of them will die before the year is over.

YOU HAVE JUST ARRIVED AT A NOTABLE RESTAURANT AND HAVE BEEN shown to a table upstairs. Your attention is immediately drawn to a Native woman standing by the second-storey window. She appears anxious; her clothing is outdated; her name is Red Feather.

You turn your head, and see a young boy wearing checkered overalls. He is running through the dining room. Where are his parents?

Then you turn back, shocked to discover a bearded man sitting across from you. He is staring straight ahead. Wait a minute, he's also wearing old-fashioned garments and has a bottle of scotch beside his dinner plate. He nods in your direction. His name is Carl.

Shaken, you glance at the menu to get your bearings. "Welcome to Greystones Inn." In that moment you realize that Greystones Inn is a highly spirited place.

Nanette and Tony Martin own Greystones Inn, a stately stone structure located in the downtown core of Orangeville, Ontario. This historic Inn is known by many locals to be inhabited by no less than eight spirits who all have some connection to the building's past.

The original proprietor of the inn was James Graham, born in 1805, in Armagh, Ireland. He immigrated to Canada at an early age and lived in what is now known as Toronto. There he married Mary Ann Campbell and moved to a farm in Amaranth in 1843.

In 1852, the census for Amaranth listed James as farmer, living in a one-storey log cabin. He was forty-seven years old and Mary Ann was thirty-six. The family was comprised of Margaret, age eleven; Ester, age ten; James, age eight; Elizabeth, age four; and John, age two. There had been a female child who died at birth in 1851.

That same year the family moved to a log dwelling in Orangeville where Greystones stands today. There, James opened a tavern. He was a tenant of Jesse Ketchum. By 1854, his future looked brighter.

Female spirit appears by the bar in Greystones Inn.

In his book entitled *Orangeville*, Wayne Townsend, the present-day curator of the Dufferin County Museum and Archives, writes of many changes and developments over the next twenty-five years.

A stone building was added in 1854 on what is currently Third Street and Broadway. It was Georgian architecture as it is today but was only about one-quarter the size of the present-day inn. The building also functioned as a stagecoach stop.

As a tavern it offered quite a variety of liquor — brandy, rye from Detroit, Malt mountain dew, Old Crow, Diamond Whiskey, and peat-packed V.R. Whiskey from Belfast, Ireland.

James's wife, Mary Ann, passed on December 2, 1858, at the relatively young age of forty-four. The Canadian census of 1861 showed James Graham as an innkeeper still, with a new wife named Margaret. They went on to have three more children, Jane, William, and George.

In 1871, Graham was still there and his landlady was Mrs. Ketchum. The inn was still open for business.

Sometime between 1876 and 1878 James purchased the building and property. Although his purchase was never officially registered, the change was noted on the assessment roll.

James died on October 7, 1879, at the age of seventy-five. His daughter Ann and her husband, Thomas Clegg, bought the property from the family. Prior to this, the Cleggs had operated a hotel in Toronto and a summer resort in Muskoka.

Thomas was thought to be a bit of a bounder and a lady's man, someone who lived by his wits. It was suggested that Thomas was the reason that the inn was eventually sold out of the family.

Red Feather was a young Native woman who worked at the inn; it was rumoured that she was the mistress of Thomas Clegg. Red Feather was possibly from the Native summer settlement situated on Purple Hill, in the area where the Orangeville hospital now stands. This Native encampment existed long after the settlement of Orangeville was established.

In 2007, Nanette and Tony Martin approached Dan Sheehan about acquiring the building and property. Sheehan had used the building for private functions. Nanette does not hesitate to acknowledge that Sheehan helped her make a dream come true. She had been in the hospitality business for more than twenty years at that point in time.

In his book, entitled *Power, Freedom and Grace*, author Deepak Chopra writes about happiness and dreams. He describes the need for us to follow our desires and look for coincidences.

This was Nanette's experience on her first visit to Greystones.

As Deepak explains, "The more we live in the state of happiness, the more we experience the spontaneous fulfillment of desire in the form of synchronicity and meaningful coincidence. In many spiritual traditions, this has been called the state of Grace. To experience grace is to find ourselves in the right place at the right time, to have the support of the laws of nature, or 'good luck.'"

Nanette could not agree more. "I had such an amazing coincidence when I first visited the building. For years my email address read 'No No Nanette.' Walking through the building I discovered a theatre poster on the wall highlighting a musical production entitled 'No No Nanette'!"

Mr Sheehan's patience and direction assisted Nanette and Tony to get their venture off the ground.

Richard Vivian, the author of an article about the inn that was published in October 2007, stated, "A bottle of scotch is placed on the second-storey table at Greystones. The bottle is placed there at the request of Carl, one of eight spirits who reside here.

"The head chef at the time, Bryan Young, had direct encounters with two of the spirits, including Carl.

"It's not known whether the name of the spirit is Carl — but that was the only name mentioned during the conversation with Young. The conversation included information about a table, located on the second floor of the restaurant."

Nanette commented, "There was never a table here before. I was trying to arrange this area in seating. I put a table here and I guess he [Carl] liked it here. It seems he does not mind sharing this area with us, as long as his table is back in this corner and reset."

Richard Vivian also said, "The table must be set for two people with a bottle of scotch."

Carl did show himself to Bryan Young. He was described as having a beard with a mustache. He said he was at the inn because of a confrontation, but failed to elaborate.

Young remarked, "I have always been able to sense that there was something up there [second floor]. Everybody that has worked here has said they could sense it."

One day Nanette decided to conduct a test to see if Carl really exists and if he actually sits at the table on the second floor by the fireplace.

"I always set that table with a black tablecloth. This time I put a small amount of baby powder on the edge of the table on top of the black linen. I left the cutlery and plates in total disarray. No one was privy to my experiment.

"I returned in a couple of hours to check the table. To my amazement the table was completely set. The cutlery and plates were in their proper place. It was perfect. The baby powder was gone. There was not a sign of anybody around."

Dan Pelton, a staff reporter with the *Orangeville Citizen* newspaper wrote an article entitled "Greystones: a spirited place to dine." In his article, he introduced the spirit named Carl.

"Should you sit down to dine at a particular table in the Greystones Inn, there's a chance you may be joined, invited or not, by a cantankerous chap with an unquenchable penchant for scotch and a wit one may find a little caustic. Management regrets to inform you that they are powerless to remove the man from the premises, but assures you that he's a nice guy, once you get to know him."

About other spirits in the building Young remarked, "Carl spoke of two women and an eight-year-old child, but did not mention the others."

Nanette says that Red Feather, a Native spirit in the inn, can be sensed throughout the building. Another spirit, dubbed Annie, is in the original section of the building, which is the bar area on the first floor. Annie seems to dislike Red Feather.

One possible reason for Annie to not like Red Feather could be that Annie was Ann Graham, the daughter of James and wife of Thomas Clegg. No love lost between a wife and a mistress!

When Nanette was preparing to open the restaurant in 2007, she hired a photographer to take some publicity photographs. Amazingly, Annie was captured on film as a full apparition standing behind the bar area.

Nanette met the sister of a woman who once lived in the building in the 1960s. This was a period when, according to Wayne Townsend in *Orangeville*, you could go to the inn to have your fortune told. Apparently this woman's sister did experience some paranormal activities.

"At the time, the woman was raising a young family. The upstairs of the building served as a living room. Their dog was terrified at times in the building. A pool table was located downstairs. The woman would often hear the pool balls moving when no one was there. The woman had to move out because she was too afraid to be alone in the building."

An artist, hired twenty years ago to redesign the second-storey room, encountered some unexplained activity. Alone in the building and painting away on the second floor, she heard a thunderous banging at the front door. She went downstairs to answer the door, but no one was there. She also said that a tall man appeared every day and looked down at her. She did finish the job.

Nanette frequently finds dimes on the floors throughout the building. The use of dimes is not uncommon when it comes to dealing with spirits. On the sea islands off the South Carolina and Georgia coast, the blended African American Gullah practitioners decorated gravesites with coins, glasses, and shells to quiet restless spirits.

Is there someone buried beneath the building at Greystones, or nearby? Is one spirit trying to quiet another? Is there an African element? Nanette believes that Red Feather might be buried behind the building.

Historically, silver dimes have been used to ward off evil spirits; if the dime turns black, it is a sure sign that one has been conjured; a good luck charm would be a penny nailed to the doorstep; pennies on the floor will please the faeries.

Thomas Clegg is felt to still be around. He was, after all, thought to be a ladies' man. Nanette thinks he still has an eye for the women.

"I wear my apron on my side, part of it covering my backside. Thomas apparently likes to hang out on the back stairs that lead from the kitchen to the upstairs banquet room on the second floor. He unties my apron to have a look at my behind."

On one occasion, Nanette went to the building before going on a trip. "I had a bad feeling about a spirit in the building. I knew it was a man.

"It is always cold on the back staircase. I was carrying some glasses to the kitchen when someone or something tripped me on the stairs. Fortunately I tumbled down the stairs without hurting myself."

There have been other occasions on the back stairs.

"I was walking by the washrooms located on the second floor and starting down the back staircase when suddenly a bottle of hand lotion came flying by me and landed at the bottom of the stairs. The bottle of hand lotion had been in the bathroom. I was shocked!"

Every Wednesday night for a month, Nanette had a very odd experience in the one dining room with a fireplace that no longer was used as a heat source. "I would walk over to the fireplace and smell wood burning. I believe 'they', as in the spirits, want to see a fire burning in the room."

Nanette took a picture of the fireplace. Looking at the photograph afterwards she noticed an orb of light floating in the air by the fireplace. In the orb was a face. Nanette was told that the face was that of Carl. He just wanted her to see him.

I decided to do some investigating myself.

One evening at Greystones, I met with a gifted "sensitive" by the name of Lori Kennelly. Lori had agreed to meet me and to tour the building to see if we could encounter any of the spirits. She felt that everyone has the gift to see the spirit world.

Before we started I asked her to share any previous experiences she had had at Greystones. She told me about the pub and office in the downstairs area of the building.

"Down in the pub and back office I experience fear. A very uncomfortable feeling as if people were punished here. A black rod [orb] shot in front of me as I was leaving the room. To me it felt like residual energy. An orb is a spirit to me. They are making themselves known to you. They are people of the past."

Lori talked about the cellar area in the lower level of the building.

"I do not feel too comfortable in the cellar. I am attracted to the wall. This is where I believe Red Feather, the Native woman is buried."

On the second floor she had had a brief encounter.

"I once got a picture of an orb where it is believed Carl sits by the fireplace. One night the lights flickered when we were upstairs. I felt as though someone was standing by me in my personal space. It was okay.

"I feel very positive here at Greystones, a very welcoming place. I have done spiritual readings here. I believe the spirits remember me.

"One time I was doing a spiritual reading on the second floor. I felt someone looking over my shoulder."

Lori concluded, "I believe there is an opening or portal here where the spirits can come and go."

The time had come for Lori, Nanette, and I to do a tour of the building together. Before we even started the tour Lori remarked, "Somebody is here right now. My ears are popping."

I waited. I did not see anything — my ears did not pop. Darn.

Lori continued, "I suddenly have a scratchy throat. A person may have passed away here. It was a heart attack. I am getting a picture of a male figure."

We went from the bar, downstairs to the lower-level pub and cellar. The men's washroom is at the bottom of the stairs.

Lori began to feel uncomfortable.

"I see a mist inside the cellar storage area. I feel very different here. Something to do with punishment."

I did not see anything; darn.

Her vision began to blur.

We heard a door slam. Someone just entered the downstairs washroom. I volunteered to check it out. Cautiously I opened the door to the men's washroom, and entered. No one was there. I left quickly!

From there we went to the pub. A female regular, so the story goes, always takes the corner table and she inevitably reports seeing a spirit by the doorway, near that washroom area.

The chandelier in the bar area began to flicker — then stopped. We stopped. Again, it flickered. We had company!

Nanette felt Thomas behind her. Thomas, who likes to play tricks.

We moved on, to another area on the lower level. There we could see the original stone foundation that supports the building. Where originally there were stairs to the outside. Now a parking lot is there by the side of the building. This, some people believe, is the burial site of Red Feather. Unfortunately Red Feather didn't make an appearance.

Back upstairs we turned into the first dining room. Lori stared, "There is something by the left side of the fireplace. It is Thomas."

We waited. Then we headed up the staircase to the second floor. As we reached the top of the stairs I was reminded what Nanette had said earlier. "A woman is felt standing at the top of the central staircase. People have felt a loss of breath as though someone was walking through them."

As we entered the dining/banquet hall, Lori said, "There is someone seated in the corner of the room."

Was it Carl?

We walked the room and returned to our starting point.

Greystones may have a host of mysterious spirits, but there is also a host of delicious dishes and we were ready.

Homemade southern crab cakes on a bed of sautéed spinach, beef tenderloin, rib eye, or strip loin, Bombay curry, and lobster.

Hauntings aside, historic Greystones Inn gets good press!

Below are some of the comments penned in the guest book:

1. "My wife and I stopped into Orangeville. After walking around we found Greystones at the eastern end of town. Clean and bright, the interior was well decorated and retained the old world charm."

2. "The server was friendly and professional. My wife had the bruschetta and said it was the freshest she had ever had. I decided on the chicken pot pie, a choice I didn't regret."

3. "My husband and I went out for dinner to celebrate our anniversary. The menu was, as always, excellent and the quality of our food was very high."

So it is also "a haunt" for determined diners! And the fare that's there will make their spirits rise! Just make sure you are not booking for thirteen.

Orillia Opera House
~ Orillia, Ontario ~

YOU ARE STANDING IN THE HISTORIC ORILLIA OPERA HOUSE, BUILT IN 1895. Over the last century, this structure has housed the opera house, council chambers, courtroom, and jail ... and a variety of spirits. For many years staff has heard a ghostly pianist at the grand piano on the stage, deep in the night. Some have heard a vaudeville act from days gone by, even accompanied by the applause of the audience. Come now and spend the night with myself and others as we search for the phantoms of the opera.

Let us first look at the story. The town of Orillia is situated at the narrows between Lake Simcoe and Lake Couchiching. The name Orillia is thought to come from the Spanish word for "shore."

The first white man known to set foot on the site of present-day Orillia was Samuel de Champlain in 1615. In 1831, the British government negotiated with the First Nations people of the area to relocate them to a village site at the Narrows. The following year settlers began to arrive.

In 1866, with a population of 750, Orillia was incorporated as a village. Six years later, in 1872, an Englishman by the name of Goldwin Smith donated half an acre to be used as a market square.

Reeve James Quinn sold some additional land in order to accommodate the market and town hall. In 1873 construction also began on a lock-up facility (jail) at the same location.

Orillia became a town in 1875. When townspeople began voicing the need for a more elaborate structure to replace the town hall and the market shed, town council passed a bylaw to raise $10,000 for that very purpose. However, no further action was taken until 1893, when another bylaw was passed to raise $15,000 by the issue of debentures.

Tenders were petitioned for the construction of the Opera House, which would include a town hall, a courtroom, and a jail. The contract was awarded to Messrs Hammond and Robinson.

By November 1893, the shell of the building was up, yet very little work had been done on the inside. Council dismissed Hammond and Robinson and took direct control of the project.

The building was eventually completed; it opened on November 4, 1895. The total cost of construction was $25,000.

The building existed in relative tranquility until one fateful night in 1915. Shortly after midnight on July 15, 1915, the fire alarm was raised; the Opera House was on fire. In less than two hours the magnificent structure was in ruins. Damage resulted in a loss of more than $30,000, according to the *Weekly Times* newspaper.

Council decided to rebuild. The grand opening took place on Thursday, March 1, 1917.

In the early days of the Opera House the public attended vaudeville acts. Boris Karloff, of Hollywood fame as Count Dracula, performed here; during the First World War the Plunkett family entertained as the "Dumbbells."

Donald Jenkins, in a story entitled "At War with Germany" said, "The Plunketts took the name, Dumbbells, from the insignia of the 3rd Division, and the name became widely known in the trenches, in London, across Canada, and even on Broadway.

"Albert, Merton, and Morley Plunkett, three brothers with good voices and histrionic ability brought fame to Orillia, their birthplace."

In a later article entitled "Movies," Jenkins explained what happened after vaudeville.

"Beginning in 1920 and continuing until 1958, the auditorium was leased and used as a cinema. In the early years of the silent films, a succession of local musicians played the piano during the showing of the film; they followed cue starts to allow them to indicate changes in mood. Mrs. Frank Gover, Eric McFadden, and Clare Clark were some of the pianists."

The existence of a secret tunnel in the Orillia Opera House has long been a topic of discussion. The stories surrounding this tunnel have created an atmosphere of intrigue and mystery.

A *Packet and Times* newspaper article published years ago stated, "It's been seventy-five years since beer barrels rumbled through the old arched tunnel, but rumours of illicit underground traffic still echo through the streets of Orillia. If you have lived in this town for any length of time you've heard about the notorious tunnel, said to link city council chambers to a den of iniquity across the street. As legend has it, the tunnel ran from the bowels of the Orillia Opera House under Mississauga Street to the basement of the building diagonally opposite, now occupied by Fred's Meat Market."

Randy Richmond in his article "The Legend of the Tunnels" states, "According to local amateur historian Wendy Hutchings, the tunnel was constructed in 1910. It ran from a brewery where Fred's is now to a malt house next door. The brewery closed in 1916, but the tunnel remained."

However, Hutchings is now sceptical. When the city dug up Mississauga Street in the early 80s, they went down ten feet. She noted, "There was no tunnel."

Richmond added, "Bill Darner, owner of Fred's Meat Market, says the tunnel was filled in during the 1940s when Mississauga Street was reconstructed." Despite various opinions, those tunnels are there in the minds of those who want to believe in them.

There is no doubt that the Orillia Opera House is haunted. In the book entitled *Phantoms of the Orillia Opera*, an unknown author penned this statement, "Perhaps because of the size and age or perhaps because of its sealed tunnels and dungeons, many feel that phantoms do exist here."

There are two distinct haunts that appear from time to time to scare the pants off all concerned:

> The first ghost is undoubtedly a musician, a pianist who delights in playing the grand piano on stage until the

very second that the anxious actor or stage hand arrives in the wings. This phenomenon has become so frequent that some people have refused to work alone in the building – not from fear, but from frustration at the constant interruptions. Whatever spirit haunts our stage at night "it" plays beautiful music, until the performers approach, then leaves the piano still humming with a final chord.

The second well-known haunt involves a local character who fell down an elevator shaft during the reconstruction of the Opera House, broke both of his legs, and was not found until three days later. He had the misfortune to fall on Friday night and was not missed over the weekend. He ultimately died as a result of his injuries and is considered to be one of the ghosts.

The author continued:

Often during the summer, our Front-of-House staff must close up the theatre very late at night. It was on just such an occasion that a harrowing incident happened a few years earlier.

Upon entering the orchestra area our Front of House Manager felt an icy blast of air, far colder than any air-conditioning. At exactly the same time, she heard ghostly laughter and applause coming out of the darkness, as if a ghostly audience was enjoying some vaudeville or comedy act long turned to dust.

She was terrified. She exited the orchestra area on a burst of eerie laughter. So afraid was she of interrupting the spirits, she backed down the many stairs to the lobby without turning on the lights and fled outside.

In January 2006, Producers Nick and Robin Poulakis and I, shot a pilot episode at the Orillia Opera House for a potential paranormal television show entitled *Haunted Heritage*. The intention was to spend the entire night, with two film crews and the lights out, in the Opera House. The second part of this project was to research the ghost stories and history of the building and then invite a well-known spiritualist to see what they could sense about the spirits and about the history of the building. Nick and Robin tracked down a popular American spiritualist, Greg Kehn, from Lily Dale, New York.

Greg had never been to Orillia nor did he know anything about the Opera House before his arrival there.

Our pilot opened with an interview of Mark Hurst, building manager of the Opera House at the time.

I sat at the piano on the stage while I questioned Mark and asked him to share his personal stories.

Mark elaborated, "I've been working here for a little over twenty years. When I first started here I would often work alone into the late hours. One night I could swear I heard someone playing the piano. I thought someone was playing a joke on me. I went to the stage area but no one was there — just the piano.

"Other staff members have heard the piano music, as well. I don't think we're all nuts."

I then asked Terri Rossiter, the house manager, if she wanted to share anything from her time there.

She replied, "There was one evening I was working here during what was called 'Phantom Night.' Several things happened that night. Cool breezes could be felt. Our technician told us that someone was whispering behind him. He was all alone.

"That night one of the ushers heard footsteps behind her as she climbed the staircase to the turret tower.

"Then at the end of the night we were all standing at the top of the stairs. A fire hose encased in a box just outside the elevator dumped itself onto the floor, but only one fold at a time right there in front of us. Now I don't have an explanation for that or know why it would happen, but it definitely happened.

"Later that evening I thought I saw someone running up the stairs. The technician and I took off upstairs after the person, but there was no one there. All the doors were locked."

Mark offered to tell the story about "the screaming shaft."

"In 1915, there was a fire in the Opera House. City officials decided to rebuild. One of the things they put in was a brand new elevator shaft. It was located just behind the stage area. On one Friday, a workman accidentally fell down the shaft. It was said he spent the weekend screaming. No one came to find him. On the Monday after he was discovered by the work crew. He had severe injuries to his legs and other parts of his body. He died shortly afterwards.

"Once in a while, when you are wandering through the building late at night, you'll hear a scream or a little moan."

We went to the basement next, where the former jail or lock-up still exists, and where the old tunnel entrance is blocked up! Larry Cotton, historian and author of *Whiskey and Wickedness* came along too.

Larry knew about the stories surrounding the booze, the tunnel and the jail and he shared them. "There is a lot of conjecture about the origin and purpose of this tunnel, but we do know it existed."

Larry drew my attention to the wall and added, "This wall is interesting because one of the stories is that the tunnel went from this building under Mississauga Street, the main street of Orillia, to a brewery on the other side of the street. Looking at the wall, we have a poured cement structure which is offset by blocks, and then we have an area that has been repaired and parged."

I wanted to know if Larry was suggesting that there might have been some town fathers, who, after a council meeting, instead of putting their coats on and going home, might have gone down to the basement area and travelled through the tunnel for a nightcap.

He said, "We can only use conjecture to link the two, but it is a possibility."

I knew he had some connection to the police force of those days.

Larry, "My great uncle was a chief constable in the town of Orillia in the period from 1897 to 1905. This area right here was the jail."

The downstairs area is now the men's washroom, without any obvious signs indicating that the area had once been a lock-up area.

Mark had some pertinent information.

"This was where five jail cells were located."

To help me get a visual, Mark drew my attention to a small opening in the wall that was covered over with plywood. Then he unscrewed the board to reveal the inside of a jail cell.

He explained, "I never knew these cells existed until I started looking at the old architectural drawings of the building. The drawings revealed an area 8x40 feet in the basement that had vanished from view. A custodian said there were jail cells sealed in by a wall. We created an opening in the wall to reveal the cells."

Spiritualist/medium Greg Kehn came to the Opera House. We toured the entire building with him and the film crew followed. We began in the main foyer. We had no idea what to expect.

Greg said, "The first thing I see is a greeter. I feel he was greeting everybody. He was really proud of everything here and what he did. I see the grey hair — the mustache. I am not sure of the size of the body."

(Our historical research revealed that a past chairman of the Management Committee Board was a grey-haired man with a mustache and self-appointed lobby greeter.)

Greg continued, "He was the one who kept things going.

"A woman's presence is coming in. I see her coming from that side [which is the right side of the lobby as you enter the building]. She is an older woman. You might term her as a ticket booth person. The lady was here forever. This woman was like a part of the building. I get a wonderful feeling here."

(Historical research indicated that past chairman and former actor Ken Brown remembers a short woman sitting on a stool at the ticket booth during the silent film era.)

I asked Greg if he could see her right at that moment.

He replied, "I see her by the doorway. She is a short lady with an old hair style and old style clothing. I don't think she could get up very quickly or do steps very well. She was right here, policing the lobby."

"Is she here all the time?" I asked him.

Greg stated, "I feel she comes and goes. When the energy of the people is here she likes to be here. She enjoys everyone being here."

Next Greg said, "Who is the gentlemen with a mission?" He stopped and then said, "Would there have been an old projector that would have had a hand crank ... It was his baby. He maintained the gears. He maintained everything to do with the mechanical operation. He would do it himself. His presence is very strong. He is often around too."

(History tells us that from the silent movie era of the roaring twenties until the late stages of the sock-hop fifties, the opera house auditorium was used as a cinema.)

Greg's next comment made me feel as though there was a whole world around me that was somehow invisible to me — no matter how hard I looked.

"Someone keeps looking over from the banister, over there. I keep getting a male. He would keep his eye on everything."

My eyes saw nothing! (Once again my historical research revealed that a man named Saul Robbins had enjoyed handing out free movie matinee tickets during Halloween. He positioned himself by the banister to keep an eye on everything.)

I commented that we seem to have a crowd with us.

He responded, "Oh, tons. We are far from being alone here."

We headed to the auditorium. At the top of the staircase Greg said, "I feel chairs moving. I feel the spirits also like to bang doors to let people know they are there; to shake people up. I get a feeling of flickering lights."

We were in the heart of the Opera House, where the people are seated for a stage production. Greg stopped and said, "I get a wonderful feeling here. I feel there was a man here who passed away from a heart attack. He was a very kind man. He is around a lot. He keeps hanging around.

"The spirits are drawn to the happiness and the excitement. They are tied into other people's experiences. They are not here all the time. They come back in to tap into the energy. It is a beautiful feeling."

I asked them if this would happen during performances.

He replied, "Yes. I feel that people have had experiences that they may or may not have recognized as spirit activity. I feel they move seats here all the time, up and down. People look but they don't see anything, but often feel that someone has just sat down behind them."

(Our historical notes from Building Manager Terri Rossiter did confirm that a patron in that exact area did pass away from heart complications during a theatre performance.)

Stories indicated that many people have heard music — during a performance — that was not part of the show!

When we reached the stage I asked Greg what he could sense.

Greg said, "The energy I feel here is of a gentleman's presence. I feel his legs were very weak. I feel he was often here in his lifetime. The energy I feel with him is that he was so supportive of everyone. I feel a very limited feeling in my legs. I feel like I'm bracing myself to walk.

"There is a woman's presence here. I want to term her 'stage-mom.' I just feel the energy. She would have been here for everything. I feel her energy as being very loving, but yet it is like, get it in order, get it right. 'This is what you need to do'. She was over to the left of the stage watching a lot. She would be directing the other people. I feel she was here and got quite old. This wasn't a young person. Her presence is very strong."

(Historical research found a match in Mrs. Frank Gover, a woman with a will of iron and who also played the piano during the silent film era.)

I asked Greg, "The spirit with the leg problems, do you sense an accident?"

Greg answered, "I feel an accident in passing. My head hurts. I feel my chest is damaged. Like a jolt to the chest. I feel someone would have tripped — not here, but in the back. I want to go back there. That's where I feel someone tripped and broke their leg or ankle. I get a pain in my right ankle and leg. I feel it was a fluke thing."

I wondered if this could this be the workman who fell down the elevator and later died of his injuries. Could Greg find the area where this event happened?

He exclaimed, "I feel if I went around that way. It is like there is an uneasiness in the floor."

We were backstage at that point. Greg pointed out that there was something above us that was not there now.

"There was some sort of walkway across there. I see two curtains. One curtain was for the audience and there was another curtain behind it."

(He was absolutely correct. There were two stage curtains. The second curtain had been painted by Isabelle McCreight. The curtain was known to be one of a very few hand-painted, fire-resistant curtains ever made.)

We then left the backstage and travelled to the administrative office. Greg got a strong sensation as we entered the area.

Greg added, "I keep seeing file boxes sitting out here, and a desk. This isn't anything like it once looked. I get a weird feeling and I see gun cabinets in the area."

Once again Greg was correct. This area was once the police administration office and storage facility.

Next stop was the dressing room in the Opera House.

"I get a strong feeling in here. It is like I could change floors. It is like something isn't solid underneath me."

I told Greg there was a very good reason for him to feel this way. He was standing over the old elevator shaft down which the workman fell! Greg felt there was a connection here to the male presence he spoke of earlier.

"I feel the energy with this person and I feel that the injuries didn't kill him immediately. He died shortly thereafter. The energy I feel with him is that he likes the physical energy of people coming into the building and he wants to be supportive and helpful. He is happy to be here because people like it here. I feel he likes to play with objects by moving or bumping things. He likes to make noise. This is his way of getting their attention. It is a very peaceful feeling that he is here. I feel his presence very strongly. Since we left the stage he has been with us the whole time. He is right there in front of us. He is standing and watching us."

All of this "invisible-to-me" reality made me a little uneasy. I asked Greg if he considered there to be an opening or portal in the building, one where any spirit might pass through.

Greg said, "I wouldn't call it a portal. I sense or feel an energy when they come through. I feel it more than I see it. I have been to some places where you can feel negative energy, but here, overall, I feel very positive energy."

We went from there to the basement.

Greg stated, "I almost feel tipsy here. My balance is off a little. I get a feeling of a bench here. I felt a door right here. It was more reinforced at one time."

We were by the small sheet of plywood that Mark had shown me before. It was to Greg's right and I asked him what he could pick up there.

He said, "I feel there was a shield on the wall at one time; not a piece of wood. I think there might have been something like metal here. I feel

I could reach through it. Something like bars. There is a feeling of confinement. I feel a little bit of heaviness. I feel someone was hurt here. I feel more than one person. A low, earthly energy is going on here. This isn't the more relaxed energy. There is more of control energy, more about limitations."

When I told Greg that this was the former jail and lock-up area with five jail cells that ran along behind the wall by the sheet of plywood, he said, "The feeling of confinement and despair goes back a long time ago. This wasn't the modern day. I don't see them wearing the weapons of today."

Further into the washroom area, Greg turned to face the wall on his left. (This is where it is believed to be the entrance area to the underground tunnel.) Greg placed his hand on the wall and closed his eyes for a few moments. Then he remarked, "Someone is teasing and saying they are not buried behind the wall." That brought a laugh and some relief!

"I get a whole other room. This room, another room, and the connection between the two, but not necessarily in the same structure — a tunnel with branches that went two ways."

(Some believe an underground tunnel was constructed in 1910 running from the basement of the opera house under the main street to the other side. At that point the tunnel forked into two directions — one branch led to the brewery and the other to a house of ill repute.)

What was the pain Greg sensed in the jail area?

Greg, "I do not believe they are earthbound spirits. They definitely died here. I feel my chest and my head hurting. I feel they went very quickly in the end.

"I feel a lot of energy around this, including controversy like 'who did what?' It is at peace now. I feel a male energy. He has progressed.

"I don't feel that the community at the time knew what was happening. A select few would have known. I feel it was actually kept quiet for a while. Then later on it was finally acknowledged."

Later Greg added to his experience in the jail.

"It is the weirdest sensation I felt there. I felt it was a political occurrence that forced them to seal things up. Something occurred behind the scenes ... like just eliminate this and there will not be a problem. I feel there is one entity that still hangs out here. They do not have the freedom to move on. They have chosen to be here. It is a choice. He is with us right now."

Greg had more impressions to share.

"I felt one building [liquor emporium] to be calm. There was no problem there. However, concerning the other building [brothel] I felt uneasy. I felt uneasy with some female energy in the basement of that building. Some abuse was going on."

(While there has been no hard evidence of a brothel, some long-time Orillia residents recall it being the Peyton Place of Orillia.)

Greg, "It was a brothel. It was the building by the right tunnel."

At the exit door, Greg spoke up. "I feel horses outside."

(The former rear of the opera house, during the early 1900s, was where the horses were tied up during the farmers' market.)

Greg, "I see two activities. I see them unloading things and bringing them in here and it was secretive. They did not want people to know for some reason. There are also some things going on with people. It is to do with the tunnel. There is interesting energy here from hidden to not hidden. Many things happened here."

As we climbed the stairs to the turret, Greg commented that he felt there were lookouts up here watching people. He described the energy as protective. (During the First World War the armed forces occupied the opera house.)

The projection room, just before the turret, has a view to the stage. There is a small cabinet space on the wall. Greg could feel the energy of hidden "things" here, perhaps alcohol.

As he stood in the turret area Greg commented, "I feel a tremendous amount of energy flow here. There are a couple of areas in the building where the energy is strong, especially here and down in the basement where you have the two doorways."

The next step was for the team so spend several hours in the opera house without the benefit of lights.

We had two groups of participants; each with their own camera man and equipment. They explored separately until they joined together at 3:45 a.m.

Director Robin Poulakis was conducting base-line readings in the building. These base-line readings consisted of taking the temperature readings and electro-magnetic field (EMF) measurements. Unusually low temperatures of high EMF readings indicate the presence of paranormal activity.

Director Nick Poulakis had placed a camera inside the one jail cell in the afternoon. He had turned the camera on and boarded up the opening.

One group headed up the stairs to the turret room. The other group went to the stage area.

The production assistant, Mathew Anderson, stopped halfway up the stairs to the turret. He heard a knocking sound. The group stopped to listen. There it was again. It sounded faintly like a door closing. We continued on and entered the turret room.

Robin's equipment registered a great and sudden change in temperature. We had company!

This was followed by a scraping sound, as though someone were moving a piece of furniture in the projection room right in front of us! Our once-calm approach morphed into tense apprehension.

Robin shouted, "What the heck was that? I just saw a flash right near the doorway."

"If there is someone there, let us know. Can you bang on something?"

All went still and we decided to leave the area.

Aha! It happened again ... fainter this time. As we returned below to the auditorium foyer, Mathew realized the door was open. I had purposely and personally closed that door on the way up! That was the sound we had heard! The opening and closing of that door!

We checked to see if it had been the other group. It was not!

Nick stated, "Maybe it [the spirit] is following us."

As we continued down, it happened again!

By now it was 3:45 a.m. and both teams joined forces to explore the basement.

In the record archives of the basement, Nick asked me about the paranormal energy associated with the jail. I told him that condemned prisoners were held in the basement until they were transported to Barrie to be "hanged until dead."

Prisoners who were hung are known to haunt their cells and sometimes courtrooms on the anniversary of their demise.

Robin said, "If there is anybody here please give us a sign."

No response.

We were now in the former lock-up area. Five sealed cells. Only one cell could be viewed through a very small opening. We could just barely see and read the names scratched on the walls within.

A tense wait revealed little until ... what! ... A shadow!

Robin yelled, "I just saw a shadow by the doorway back to the basement!"

Jackie Leblanc heard a moan.

Our energy soared and then ... footsteps ... and we were rendered silent!

Robin spoke up, "I heard that!"

Jackie said, "That moan was pain."

More footsteps.

Robin said, "Show yourself!"

More noise ... the temperature dropped.

Someone said, "There's something here."

Jackie freaked.

Cameras were focused and the temperature guide drew us to the lock-up cell.

The temperature dropped again ... four degrees Celsius!

Nick said, "Let's leave and see if it follows."

We counted. Everyone was there. We left for the theatre.

There were no more "happenings."

Blair Agnew was on duty the night we were filming. He had to lock up after we all left.

Blair, "When everyone was packing up, Terry Boyle mentioned to me that the group had encountered a spirit in the basement. I recalled that we had advised the spirit to not follow us home."

Blair continued, "Everyone had left. All the lights were out. I packed up my own car. I returned to the building to set the alarm and discovered a door was still open in the basement. The door had to be closed before I could set the alarm. In the back of my mind I remembered there was something down there! So I went downstairs, checked it out, closed the door, and felt okay. Then I just got spooked. Something came over me and I started running, putting my hand up and shouting 'stay back.' I got to the door, locked it, set the alarm, and fled. I was shaken up ... and ... I was frightened!"

Discovery Harbour

~ Penetanguishene, Ontario ~

OCCASIONALLY, WHEN A TRAVELLER SETS OUT TO DISCOVER THE WORLD, they may unexpectedly open a doorway to the mysterious world of spirits, where an altered reality can affect the senses.

Penetanguishene is steeped in Native history. Located in Simcoe, County northwest of Barrie, on the southern tip of Georgian Bay, it was once home to the Huron (Wyandot) who settled there in semi-permanent villages. The name Penetanguishene is believed to be a Wyandot word meaning "place of the white rolling sands."

In 1793, John Graves Simcoe, the first Lieutenant-Governor of Upper Canada, visited the district and saw the potential here for a naval base.

Although Penetanguishene harbour had long been a centre of activity for traders, when John Graves Simcoe proposed to build a military road from Kempenfeldt Bay on Lake Simcoe to terminate at Penetanguishene, its future as a town was born.

The road, which actually originated in York (Toronto), was not built until 1814. Simcoe's main intention was to use the bay at

Penetanguishene to shelter warships to protect British interests on lakes Huron, Erie, and Michigan.

Settlement was slow until 1817, when the construction and establishment of a military base began. There was a need for a strong naval presence on Lake Huron should hostilities be renewed with the United States. However, the Rush-Bagot agreement between Britain and the United States restricted the number of active warships that either side could have on the Great Lakes. Therefore, the British warships *Tecumseh* and *Newash* required a harbour where they could be decommissioned and maintained in a state of readiness should trouble flare up.

By 1820, the base was home to more than seventy personnel, including sailors, civilian workers, officers, and a military guard.

The naval establishment was also home to more than twenty vessels. As the threat of American invasion diminished, regular soldiers were recalled to England and replaced by half-pay officers who brought their families with them and supplemented their pensions by farming part time.

The early population included English and French fur traders, Métis, fishermen, and farmers.

The entrance to Discovery Harbour naval base, 1817

In 1834, the navy closed down operations. The base became just a military establishment with military drill and garrison routines. An impressive officers' quarters and a soldiers' barracks were built. The gradual withdrawal of British troops from the Canadian colonies meant significant change for frontier posts like Discovery Harbour.

From 1846–51, the role of the military at Penetanguishene was filled by the Royal Canadian Rifle Regiment. By 1851, the expense of operating it could not be maintained. The military establishment was left to the care of pensioners. In 1856, the establishment ceased operations for good.

In 1859, the former naval and military garrison became a juvenile reformatory for boys. Youth were sent here to undergo a program of discipline and labour intended to teach them skills and responsibilities.

The former officers' quarters became the warden's residence and the old soldiers' barracks was redesigned into the inmates' dormitory. The chaplain occupied the former home of Adjutant James Keating.

At the turn of the century, the elimination of the reformatory system marked another change for the former garrison. In 1904, the entire complex became a hospital for the insane. This would lead to many energy imprints or residual energy on site.

Today, the British establishment at Discovery Harbour is comprised of several buildings that were reconstructed to the historic blueprints. The Officers' Quarters is the only surviving structure from the military garrison. The interior of the building is furnished to represent the 1840s period.

Let us open the door to the past and to the mysterious world of spirits; let us have a tour of Discovery Harbour.

Picture this. The King's Wharf Theatre is the first building on your left. It has many of the architectural features of the original Naval Storehouse that once stood there.

The Naval Storehouse was a three-storey structure that housed an eighteen-month supply of provisions, medical stores, bedding and clothing. Rigging and sails from the warships were maintained in the storehouse, as well as the ships' guns and other small arms. Gunpowder was stored on a nearby island, which was renamed Magazine Island. Beyond the storehouse were the docking facilities for the ships.

The naval pier at Discovery Harbour.

Just prior to the reconstruction of the storehouse into the King's Wharf Theatre, the first floor was filled with barrels and coils of rope. A visitor approached a staff supervisor one day and claimed to be a psychic. She felt that something bad had happened in this building. She was walking around and then she suddenly stopped at a spot near the south wall stairs, in front of the cleat rack. She declared that this was the spot where an accident had happened. Someone dropped a heavy object that they were carrying and broke an arm or a leg.

Just up the road on the right is the quartman's office. The quartman was Robert Adams. His job was to oversee civilian personnel and ensure that the vessels and buildings remained in a good state of repair.

Just across the way was the office of the clerk-in-charge. This clerk was responsible for participating in the regular mustering (roll-call) of the men, marking all entries and discharges, and completing pay bills and pay lists.

Further up on the left is a structure that housed the sailors. A regular complement of six sailors was posted at Penetanguishene. The sailors were responsible for the maintenance of the rigging and sails of the decommissioned ships. The assistant surgeon was housed in the building next to the sailors' barracks.

Reconstructed buildings at Discovery Harbour.

In 1819, the assistant surgeon was Clement Todd. He lived here with his wife Eliza. While the working men of the base received treatment at a remote Naval Hospital, officers had the privilege of being received at the surgeon's home.

The good surgeon would implement common treatments of the nineteenth century, such as bloodletting by lancet or leeches, and preparing and administering pills and medicine.

A little farther down the road to the right is the cemetery. Cemeteries are notorious for spirit activity. Visitors to graveyards often hear voices when no one is there or see a misty form near a grave stone. Cemeteries are eerie, lonely places where very few people ever bother to venture to.

The cemetery at Discovery Harbour has many original tombstones. One grave is that of Rosanna McCabe, a young girl believed to have been from Penetanguishene. She died in April, 1839, at the age of ten. It is believed that she died of scarlet fever. Her uncle was a soldier at the garrison.

Another grave is that of John and Samuel McGarraty, brothers and soldiers, buried together in the cemetery. Local historian A.C. Osborne shares what happened to these two brothers.

"It was this regiment which furnished the Long Woods ... to march to early times was a tedious and laborious one. On the last day of a weary march (third day since leaving York (Toronto) of thirty-five miles, they had just reached the Long Woods below Wyebridge, when one of the brothers became ill and fell out of line. His elder brother chose to keep him company.

"The detachment pushed on, anxious to reach their destination. Darkness set in, and when a relief squad returned next morning, both brothers were found dead.

"Being the month of June, with very sultry weather and clouds of mosquitoes, the searching soldiers felt that one had died from illness and exhaustion, the other from fear and thirst, as they were found some distance apart."

Past the cemetery, on the same side of the path, stands the Commanding Officer's House. At one time Captain Samuel Roberts supervised all aspects of the garrison. He served as magistrate as well as approving estimates and transactions. Apparently Captain Roberts and his wife have remained to oversee the operations of the garrison in the twenty-first century.

In 1986, one day at dusk, one of the male tour guides at Discovery Harbour was walking back to the Visitors Centre, when he happened to catch some movement at the Roberts' house. He saw a lady dressed in a long, white gown, similar to a dress that Mrs. Roberts might have worn. The lady was waving a handkerchief to him from a closed window upstairs. Thinking it was another employee dressed in costume and playing a prank on him, he proceeded up the hill towards the dwelling. As he looked at the house again he noticed the lady was no longer visible. He rushed to the door of the house but it was locked. There was no sign of anyone within the area, which was enclosed by a five-foot-high palisade fence.

There was no way a woman wearing a long gown could have climbed over the palisade. The guide unlocked the door to the house and entered. There was no one inside.

The Naval Surveyor's House is the next building to visit. This is home to a male spirit. The home was once occupied by Lieutenant Henry Wolsey Bayfield.

In 1815, the Royal Navy decided that there was a need for professional charts for their commanders on the lakes. Bayfield, who was a talented hydrographer, was assigned to go to Lake Huron and chart that body of water. He would eventually go on to chart Georgian Bay as well.

Perhaps he's still on assignment!

During the fall education program of 1987 an employee required a couple of artifacts from the Bayfield house in order to set up some pro-grammes that morning. She arrived at the dwelling, unlocked the front door, and entered the front room. To her surprise, she caught sight of a man in nineteenth-century gentlemen's attire. He was sitting in a chair in Bayfields' bedroom. Before she could think, the man stood up, took a step, and disappeared right before her eyes!

Bayfield? Maybe.

The next stop on the right is the boat shop. Here the shipwrights at Discovery Harbour performed the ongoing maintenance and restoration of the smaller, historic watercraft.

Left from here, and down another road, is the home meant for the Adjutant, also still occupied!

In 1828, James Keating arrived at the garrison to take on the duties of fort adjutant. He was accompanied by his wife Jane, and three children. Two more children were subsequently born there.

The role of the adjutant included attending on the commanding officer to receive and implement soldier's orders for the day, conducting military drills, inspecting regiments, and assuming responsibility for the appearance and instruction of non-commissioned officers and men.

James died in 1849. His wife, Jane, and the children continued to live there until 1856 when the military base closed down. The home remained standing until it was destroyed by fire in 1913.

The current structure is based on original photographs and is con-structed around the restored double fireplace and chimney.

According to Traver Gammell, in an article entitled "Ghost Tales and Weird Stories of the Garrison" the Keating House has had its fair share of hauntings.

"Like the bedroom in the mess servants' room, the upstairs east window facing the Visitors Centre is always open. No matter how often it is closed the night before, it is always open later that night or in the morning. It must be kept in mind that the window is locked when it is closed, the same as the building is at the end of the day."

In the afternoon of July 1989, the historical interpreter heard something. She was working in the kitchen, mixing cookie batter. It was a cold, gloomy day. The rain set the mood for the day. Not many visitors had ventured out. She heard footsteps on the second floor. Was there a visitor upstairs? She couldn't recall anyone entering the building; nevertheless, she called out, 'Hello'. The footsteps stopped. No one replied.

Her rational mind said it was an animal in the walls, but it happened again — more footsteps. This time there was another sound that could be heard. It sounded like someone was dragging a heavy object, like a box or a chest, across the upper floor.

That was it. She was determined to investigate. Drumming up her courage, she climbed the stairs to the second floor. She looked in both rooms and underneath the beds. She even tried knocking on the walls. She could not make the sound she had heard!

Feeling very uneasy, she returned downstairs and called for assistance of another interpreter. Together they searched the entire house, but found absolutely nothing. She never heard the sounds again.

According to Dell Taylor, a group leader at the historic site of Sainte-Marie among the Hurons in Midland, the Keating home is very active with several spirits coming and going. For the past four years Dell has conducted a ghost walk tour at Discovery Harbour. He had more to say regarding the paranormal activity at the Keating House.

"On the last ghost walk, we encountered some very disturbing spirits in the Keating House. The spirits didn't understand what we were doing there. Several staff members on the tour started to experience severe pains in their back. Some people described the pain as a burning sensation."

The experience went unexplained!

Beyond the Keating House is the Parade Square. Here the roll-calls and inspections of the troops took place. Drills were performed at least four times a day. The soldiers were housed in a large two-storey, stone barracks that stood near the Officers' Quarters beside the Parade Square.

Official rule allowed that six out of every one hundred soldiers could have wives and children accompany them. This was not the case in Penetanguishene and there were not as many restrictions judging by the large numbers of women and children listed.

The Parade Square and the Officers' Quarters are the areas with the most intense spirit activity.

The Officers' Quarters served as a residence for the officers of the garrison. It was built to accommodate three officers, but was generally occupied by only one or two officers, plus a mess man and a servant. One of the most important activities of the building was the entertainment of senior garrison personnel and distinguished visitors from the surrounding area.

On the third weekend of July, in 1991, a female visitor stepped back in time, a witness to the past. Discovery Harbour was hosting a military re-enactment and several of the volunteer re-enactors had camped overnight in tents on the Parade Square. This included the photographer, whose husband was to be involved in the battle the next day.

Traver Gammell wrote, "Unable to sleep, she awoke at about 5:30 a.m. to use the washroom near the Officers' Quarters. There was enough light that she could see without the use of a flashlight. Approaching the washrooms, she was startled by the sight of two soldiers in full regalia standing at the southeast corner of the Officers' Quarters. The two were deep in the middle of a conversation and did not seem to notice her."

Obviously the woman thought they were members of the re-enactment group who had arrived earlier. She was mistaken.

Officer's Quarters, dining room where sherry glasses suddenly appear

Gammell continued, "As she walked a few steps towards the two soldiers, she realized that she could actually see through them. At this point the two soldiers stopped their conversation, looked at her, and then turned around and walked along the east wall of the building."

As the photographer watched the two soldiers round the northeast corner, she was intent on following them. She turned the corner but the two were no longer to be seen; they had vanished!

She explained later that there was no place where the two soldiers could have hidden. She searched for the two soldiers all weekend. No one on site had uniforms to match the uniforms of those two soldiers she had observed. Did she step back in time or is the quantum theory of "'everything' happening at the same time" a real possibility?

The Officers' Quarters certainly present some opening to another dimension of space and time. The interior of the dwelling has its share of apparitions. One afternoon in the fall of 1988, the assistant curator, Mary Skinner and employee Mary Mandley were wrapping textiles in acid-free paper. The shutters in the mess hall were opened to let in the sunshine. The main door of the Officers' Quarters was also open to enjoy the warm day. In the background there was the sound of birds chirping, the wind, and motor boats across the bay.

Gammell wrote, "All of a sudden, a cloud blocked the sun, darkening the room. All outdoor noises ceased to be heard. The curator and her employee felt an almost electrical presence in the air as the hair on their necks stood up. A white, filmy cloud floated from the pantry to the servant's hall."

Both women declared that there was no possible way that the white cloud could have been smoke.

On one summer evening in the 1970s, the interpreter/education officer had a fright while working in the upstairs offices of the Officers' Quarters. Suddenly he felt a chill in the room and an odd feeling enveloped him. It was like sensing someone near you, but you can't see them; of being watched by a phantom.

Then a stern and disembodied voice asked what he was doing there and told him to "get out."

He did indeed leave and quickly, too, and never felt the same about the building after that experience.

A female employee claimed to hear creaking on the second floor while working there alone. She described the noise as the sound of a chair rocking back and forth. Thinking that another employee might be playing a trick on her, she went upstairs to catch them. She was shocked to discover no one was there. There wasn't even a rocking chair! She closed and locked the door to the second floor and returned to her work. Soon the rocking sound began again.

It is a common complaint. For years employees have heard knocking, banging, and creaking noises emanating from the second floor.

Could it be Private Drury?

James Drury of the 15th Regiment was not happy; on December 31, 1836, New Years Eve, Drury was ordered to do guard duty at the Officers' Quarters. He wanted to celebrate in the company of his wife and child and left reluctantly to do his duty.

He was to be there until dawn. It was a frigid night to stand duty. Drury periodically stepped into the kitchen to warm himself, hoping he would not be caught by an officer. On one trip in, he noticed a bottle of liquor and thought a quick nip would do no harm. The evening began to pass more easily for the private as repeated trips to the kitchen became repeated trips to the bottle.

His duty by the stairs was no longer an unpleasant chore — he was content and warm. In fact, Private Drury no longer cared if he was caught by an officer for being drunk.

At some point during the night, Drury slipped to the ground and fell asleep in the snow; he was discovered in the morning by an officer. It no longer mattered that he was drunk — he was dead.

Employees working at the Officers' Quarters also experience the movement of objects during the night, such as a sherry glass moved from the ante-room to the senior officers' bedroom. Other items go missing and do not reappear for some time. Where do they go?

In December of 1989, during an early thaw, the Officers' Quarters experienced high humidity. To protect artifacts from mould growth, two employees packed the items into boxes and transported them to the drier climate of the Visitors Centre.

One box, containing Native war club, a flask, and a stirrup hitcher, went missing during the transfer. According to Gammell, a thorough search on both floors of the Officers' Quarters and in other locations, a search that lasted three weeks, turned up nothing.

"One afternoon an employee stood in the mess hall and in frustration, called out, 'Ok ghosts, where did you put the darn box?' That inspired one more search for the missing box. When the door to the second floor was opened, there, at the top of the stairs, was the box."

There was another environmental story in the fall of 1989. To help keep the climate of the building stable, it was decided to leave the furnace off in the Officers' Quarters for the winter. All employees were informed of this procedure — do not touch the thermostat.

In January, a group of architects arrived at the site to determine possible solutions for preserving the structure. As the group entered the Officers' Quarters, a blast of warm air struck them. The thermostat had been turned on high. The staff denied touching the thermostat. It was turned down but was back on high the very next morning.

Sometimes there is evidence of movement through time. This is true at Discovery Harbour.

This conclusion is possible in the servant's bedroom in the Officers' Quarters. No matter how many times the bed has been made in this room, the next morning the bed looks as though someone has slept in it, on top of the covers.

Bed in Officers' Quarters still being used

Gammell pointed out, "It must be kept in mind that there is a barrier to prevent visitors from entering the room and trying out the bed.

"Some staff claim that not only do they see an impression in the middle of the bed, but also at the foot of the bed. In one case the impression looked as though someone had been sitting there, leaving what looked to one employee as buttock prints."

There is no question that a doorway into another dimension exists at Discovery Harbour, an extraordinary doorway with a disorienting overlay of time. Be prepared to explore and make discoveries if you decide to travel to Discovery Harbour!

Bay Monster - Native Folklore of our Sacred Landscape

~ Parry Sound, Ontario ~

FOLKLORE, MYTHS, AND LEGENDS WERE ONCE TRADITIONAL NARRATIVE, but over time, the stories became idealized and eventually came to symbolize mysterious truths surrounding our sacred landscape and our very existence.

To believe in the stories was to believe in the supernatural world, where one could touch knowledge and power. These stories and the sacred landscape are still here with us. All you have to do is feel their truth ... and see.

A ready connection to the sacred landscape and to the knowledge and power of life around us is through the stories of Native peoples, particularly the stories passed down locally from our own early Native peoples.

"They [the Ojibwa Indians of Parry Island] lived much nearer to nature than most white men, and they looked with a different eye on the trees and the rocks, the water and the sky," wrote Diamond Jenness of the National Museum of Canada, in 1929. "They were less materialistic, more spiritually minded, than Europeans, for they did not picture any great chasm separating mankind from the rest of creation, but interpreted everything around them in much the same terms as they interpreted their own selves."

While researching for a report titled the "The Ojibwa Indians of Parry Island, Their Social and Religious Life," Jenness learned that according to them, man consisted of three parts, a corporeal body (*wiyo*) that decays and disappears after death; a soul (*udjitchog*) that travels after death to the land of souls in the west, ruled by Nanibush; and a shadow (*udjibbom*) that roams about on earth but generally remains near the grave.

"The soul is located in the heart and is capable of travelling outside the body for brief periods, although if it remains separate too long the body will die," Jenness explained. "The soul is the intelligent part of man's being. The soul is also the seat of the will."

The shadow is slightly more indefinite than the soul. It is located in the brain, but like the soul, the shadow often operates apart from the body.

"In life, it [the shadow] is the 'eyes' of the soul, as it were, awakening the latter to perception and knowledge," Jenness stated. "When a man is travelling, his shadow goes before or behind him. Normally it is in front, nearer to his destination. There are times when a man feels that someone is watching him, or is near him, although he can see no one. It is his shadow that is warning him, trying to awaken his soul to perceive the danger."

The shadow is invisible, but sometimes it allows itself to be seen under the same appearance as the body. This is why you often think you see someone who is actually miles away.

In 1929, Wasauksing (Parry Island) resident Francis Pegahmagabow shared this story about the shadow: "My two boys met me at the wharf yesterday evening and accompanied me to my house. Some time before our arrival, my sister-in-law looked out of the window and saw the elder boy pass by. It was really his shadow that she saw, not the boy himself, for we must have been nearly a mile away at the time."

Many Ojibwa living on Parry Island in the 1920s still believed that all objects had life, and life was synonymous with power. Just as man's power comes from his intelligence, his soul — so does the power of the animal, the tree, and the stone.

"Long ago the *manidos*, or supernatural powers, gathered and summoned a few Indians through dreams, giving them power to fly through the air to the meeting-place," Mr. Pegahmagabow explained. "The Indians [their souls] travelled thither, and the manidos taught them about the supernatural world and the powers they had received from the Great Spirit. Then, they sent the Indians home again."

The Parry Island Ojibwa found authority for their belief in a world of supernatural beings around them, beings who are part of the natural order of the universe no less than man himself, whom they resemble in the possession of intelligence and emotions. Like man, they too, are male or female and in some cases have families of their own. Some are friendly to the Native peoples, others are hostile.

According to the Museum report of 1929: "There are manidos everywhere, or there were until the white man came, for today, the Indians say, most of them have moved away.

"Occasionally, the Parry Islanders speak of a *Maji Manido*, Bad Spirit, referring either to some lesser being malevolent to man, most commonly the great serpent or water spirit. Apparently, the chief enemies to man are the water-serpents, which can travel underground and steal away a man's soul. If lightning strikes a tree near a Native person's wigwam [home] it is the thunder-manido driving away some water-spirit that is stealing through the ground to attack the man or his family. The leader of all water-serpents is Nzagima."

One had to be very careful of protecting the soul, Jenness points out.

"Until quite recently; and perhaps even now in certain families, adolescent boys and girls were compelled to fast for a period in order to obtain a vision and blessing from some manido," he noted. "Parents gave their children special warning against a visitation from the great serpent, which might appear to them in the front of a man and offer its aid and blessing. A boy or girl who dreamed they received a visit from a snake should reject its blessing and inform their father who would bid their return and seek a second visitation, since the evil serpent never repeats its overtures once they have been rejected. If a snake appears in another dream the boy or girl may safetly accept its blessing. But if he incautiously accepts a blessing from the evil serpent he will deeply rue it afterwards, for sooner or later he or his family will have to feed it with their souls and die."

John Manatuwaba, a seventy-year-old Ojibwa in 1929, recalled a family who fed their soul to the serpent, "A Parry Island couple had three children, two boys who died very young and a [third] child that died at birth. Two years ago the serpent swallowed the man's soul. The woman then confessed that in her girlhood she had accepted a blessing from the evil serpent."

"I recall the tales about the water-serpent," stated a Native resident of Parry Island today. "It was told to us to keep the kids from going out in deep water. This kept the children safe.

"I have heard that the water-serpent lives in Three Mile Lake and travels underground to Hay Bay. It was told to us that when a south wind blows and the water becomes murky the serpent is moving in the water."

According to another resident, a group of young children encountered the water-serpent in the 1950s on Parry Island. The creature was snake-like and had legs. It could travel through the forest as well as the water.

One Native elder on the island, when asked about the water-serpent, reinforced the belief that the creature is actually a spirit.

There are other spirits that inhabit the district, such as the little people called the *Memegwesi*, she said. They are friendly manidos, or rather a band or family of manidos. They may play pranks on the people, but never harm them. In the early part of the last century a Parry Island native on his way to Depot Harbour saw a Memegwesi going down a creek. It had the outline of a man, but only its face was visible, the body being concealed beneath a huge growth of whiskers.

John Manatuwaba, the seventy-year-old Ojibwa in 1929, recalled this encounter with the Memegwesi, "At the north end of Parry Sound, in what white men call Split Rock channel, there is a crag known to the Indians as Memegwesi's crag. Some Natives once set night lines there, but their trout were always stolen.

"At last one of the men sat up all night to watch for the thief. At dawn he saw a stone boat approaching, manned by two Memegwesi. One [was] a woman; the other was bearded like a monkey. The watcher awakened his companions and they pursued the stone boat, which turned and made for the crag. Just as the thieves reached it the woman turned around and called to the Indians, 'Now you know who stole your trout. Whenever you want calmer weather give us some tobacco, for this is our home'. The boat and its occupants then entered the crag and disappeared,"

Manatuwaba related. "The Indians still offer tobacco to these Memegwesi whenever they pass their home."

Jenness also discovered there are two kinds of invisible Indians, both closely akin to manidos, "One kind has no name; the other is called *bagudzinishinabe* or 'Little Wild Indian.' To see an individual of either kind confers the blessing of attaining old age."

The bagudzinishinabe are dwarfs that do no harm, but play innumerable pranks on human beings. Though small, no larger in fact than a little child, they are immensely strong. Sometimes they shake the poles of a wigwam, or throw pebbles on its roof; or they steal a knife from a man's side and hide it in his lodge. Often a person will eat and eat and still feel unsatisfied. He wonders how he can eat so much and still be hungry, but the dwarfs, unseen, are stealing the food from his dish.

Occasionally you hear reports of their guns, but cannot see either the dwarfs or their tracks. Yet, Francis Pegahmagabow stated that he once saw their tracks, "like those of a tiny baby," on a muddy road on Parry Island.

A few years ago a Native person camping on the island awoke in the morning to discover tiny, child-like tracks alongside her tent.

In 1976, a Rosseau area resident who was studying with Native elders encountered the little people.

"This one day I was in a beechnut forest south of Algonquin Park and I had stopped to eat some nuts," he said. "Afterwards I sat down in a glade near a babbling brook. I dozed off. Suddenly I woke up and caught a glimpse of a creature about ten feet away. At that moment it ducked behind a tree. Both of us were surprised to see each other. Then another creature appeared in the distance followed by another one to my right. I had never seen such a creature in my life. They were short, approximately two feet tall. Short mousy brown hair covered their entire body. They stood upright on their hind legs. Their front legs were shorter. I recall their long, rabbit-like ears that hung straight down their back. I had the feeling their ears could rise up like a rabbit in an alert position. The creature's eyes were set in the front of their face. The eyes were quite expressive. The nose was flat. They had no tail.

"They communicated telepathically, by way of images, leaving you with a solid impression."

"Then they led me over to the creek. They communicated that this was a special place for them. It was here that they would adjust the stones in the stream to create certain tones that would help them raise their consciousness. They told me that the lower the tone, the greater the level of consciousness.

"They communicated to me that they like tobacco and to bring some the next time, their favourite food was red squirrel."

These mysterious stories help to introduce the possibilities of seeing our world in a new way, to awaken us to the magic and enchantment lurking in all four directions, to engage our souls.

There is a tradition to ponder. When you meet a person on the road, never address them until you have passed them; then your soul and their soul will continue on their separate ways and only your bodies and shadows remain to converse. If there should be a disagreement between you it will pass away quickly, for your souls will be unaffected.

A Scent of Roses

~ Madoc, Ontario ~

IN THE STONY, UNYIELDING HILLS OF MARMORA, ONTARIO, UNTOLD numbers gather from around the world to make a pilgrimage to Greensides' Farm. Beneath a canopy of trees, amongst rugged rock outcroppings and in open fields, people kneel, pray, sing, hold hands, and even prostrate themselves as they wait for a sign from the Blessed Mary. Her divine presence can be sensed there — a fragrant scent of roses, a waft of incense, a beam of light across your path or a sudden gust of wind. She may even appear wearing a white veil and cape. Her presence is alchemical, known to have changed a silver rosary to a gold one. Her message may unlock the sacred mysteries of your own life.

She could appear to you.

On June 24, 1981, in the evening, six children climbed up Cornica hill near a small village in what was once Yugoslavia, the village of Medjugorje. An apparition of a beautiful young woman with a little child in her arms appeared in front of them. She gestured to the children to come closer but they were too frightened and then she disappeared.

The following day the children agreed to meet at the same place and time to see if she would appear again.

Immediately there came a flash of light. Once again she appeared, this time without a child. She was smiling and joyful. Once again her hands gestured for the children to come closer. This time they ventured forward and soon fell to their knees in prayer. "Our Father, Hail Mary and Glory Be." They knew her to be the Virgin Mary and she left the children with these words, "God be with you, my angels."

When the children asked if they would see her again the next day she nodded and vanished.

On the third day the children and now others encountered a light that flashed ahead three times. They all believed it to be a sign of the presence of Mary. This time she appeared higher up. She was as radiant as ever.

Some older village women, concerned about the possibility of an evil spirit, had advised the girls to carry holy water and splash it in the direction of the vision and state, "If you are Our Blessed Mother, please stay, and if you are not, go away."

This they did and Mary smiled and remained with the children. One child asked for her name. She replied, "I am the Blessed Mary."

It has been recorded that the Virgin Mary met with the children on eight separate occasions between June and December of 1982. Her mission was to reveal to the group ten secrets to be shared later at an appropriate time. She still appears in Medjugorje.

In 1990 John and Shelagh Greensides travelled to Medjugorje. During their pilgrimage Shelagh felt the presence of the Blessed Mother. To her it felt like a little bit of heaven. John became emotional when he visited St. James Church in Medjugorje. Tears flowed and, before the statue of the Virgin Mary, he stated, "Use me as you wish. You can have everything I have. Do as you want with me."

John had no idea what was in store for him and Shelagh. The farm they had purchased in 1972 in Marmora, Ontario, would soon become the second Medjugorje!

In 1991, the Greensideses decided to plan a day of prayer and thanksgiving for the tenth anniversary of the apparition of Mary in Medjugorje with friends they had made when they toured there in 1990.

Sister Alice Johnson, author of the book, *Marmora Canada: Is Our Blessed Mother Speaking Here to Her Children?* writes, "after the decision was made to celebrate the anniversary of Medjugorje, Shelagh and her daughter Ann-Marie were inspired with the thought of making the Way of the Cross throughout the old cow path that goes through the wooded land on the farm.

"A friend, Eleanor Lynch donated the fourteen stations, which she acquired from a local nursing home. With some wonderful friends they cut branches and bush along the cow trail, and discovered a natural hill of Calvary beyond the Fourteenth Station."

On the day of the event, June 23, 1991, the Greensideses were overwhelmed when nearly 200 people arrived to pray. The first sign of Mary appeared that night.

According to John Greensides, "At 6:30 p.m. a woman in the group gazed up at the sun and experienced a miracle. She told us to look up. She watched the sun spin and then tails of light appeared. The sun looked like a white disk and it moved closer. We gazed at it for half an hour. I got down on my knees to give thanks. We all know you can't look at the sun like that normally. Only the creator can be that close to the sun."

Stacy Kyle, the fourteen-year-old granddaughter of the Greensideses, was present that night. She tells it this way. "Immediately everyone glanced over at the sun and began staring. With my first glance it was amazing for there was no strain at all to the eyes. It looked as if there was a black disk blocking the harmful rays of the sun. Then I noticed it spinning very, very fast with a yellowish glare surrounding it. Suddenly it stopped spinning, but a faint up and down movement was noticeable. It seemed to be dancing gaily and others claimed it was changing colours. Then I put on a pair of sunglasses. I noticed the sun was pure white and it looked like the host."

Marg Monk in an article entitled, "Marmora ReIllusions Or Real?" highlights her experience that evening. "We were sitting on the lawn facing east, when it happened. The miracle of the sun! "Helen happened to turn in the other direction. 'Look! Look at the sun! And we witnessed the gorgeous sphere, with our bare eyes, every colour, whirling, dancing, pulsating, its colours changing unbelievably, a large halo of deepest pink encircling it, then changing to a halo of gold which even reflected to the grass at our feet."

Others that evening claimed they saw the Blessed Mother and Jesus in the sun.

According to written reports from Medjugorje, people experience similar observations of the sun when Mary appears. John Greensides adds, "The next day an overpowering scent of incense could be smelled anywhere along the stations. The scent was very illusive. My son experienced the beautiful fragrance of roses between the Thirteenth and Fourteenth Stations."

Word spread quickly to various church groups about these events occurring at Greensides' Farm. On September 29, 1991, Jo-Ann Perry decided to drive out to the farm. She wasn't sure why, but she felt the need to go. She adds, "I felt very happy, sitting amongst the beauty of nature, praying and not even knowing why I was there. Then we began the Stations of the Cross. It was such a beautiful experience as we all did our own personal pilgrimage through the woods. After each station, as we started to the next, I would look around and the faces surrounding me were always different. Where were all these people coming from?"

Miracles occur at many of the Stations of the Cross at Greensides' Farm

Jo-Ann was not prepared for what happened next. "It was at the Thirteenth Station that I was deeply moved. As Christ spoke his words to me I felt a multitude of emotions swelling up inside me. And when I replied: I beg you, Lord, help me accept the partings that must come — from friends who go away, my children leaving home ... I started to cry, beyond my control. The tears and the sobbing would not stop. My friend was concerned but she put her arm around me and I welcomed her comfort. I was also frightened and embarrassed.

"What if I was losing control? I kept thinking pull yourself together — but I continued to cry and finally just let it all come out."

Later that evening, Jo-Ann and her friend, on route to their car, observed people looking at the sky. She describes what they saw. "We looked up and I saw the sun and it started to be covered up with a map-like design. I thought it must be the branches of a tree getting in the way, so I moved to a more open space. But it happened again. After much apprehension, I resigned myself to stand there and I watched as this map-like design covered the whole sun. Then this map-like figure began to pulsate, like a heartbeat. This lasted for quite a few minutes and I will never forget what I saw. It was a miracle — a sign — we were supposed to be there and this was the sign."

Veronica Garcia, a visionary from Denver, Colorado, saw the first recorded apparition of the Blessed Mother at Greensides' Farm on June 25, 1992. Sister Alice writes, "She saw Her [The Virgin Mary] a few times during this visit. Our Lady's message to Veronica on that day was as follows: 'I've come to be your light in the darkness, my children. I have heard all of your wants, your needs, your hopes, and your love. You must learn this important lesson, my angels. It is when you turn your thoughts from your own personal wants and needs and strive towards helping my other children with their wants and needs. It is then you will discover the will of God for your life.'"

In August of 1992, Dory Tan, a resident of Mississauga, Ontario, arrived at the farm with a group of friends. At the Fourteenth Station she saw a heart beating in the large cross. As the group followed the Rosary Path, Dory asked her husband Henry for her sunglasses. Henry was unable to locate them. They asked the others to continue on and Dory and Henry returned to the Way of the Cross. There, at the Tenth Station, were Dory's sunglasses. Sister Alice describes what happened next. "Dory's sunglasses lay on the ground as though they had been deliberately placed there. The couple knelt and completed the Joyful Mysteries. When she stood and reverently raised her hands to touch the Tenth Station, the sun seemed to come right down to Dory, and in the sun she saw a white rosary. She knew nothing about Medjugorje or the miracle of the sun. Dory knelt down, crying, not understanding what was happening to her. When they continued along the Rosary Path, Dory saw a ray of bright light ahead of them, as though guiding them."

The same month the Virgin Mary appeared at the Eleventh Station to a twelve-year-old girl. When she looked up it was bright all around and everything appeared as gold. Mary manifested in a white veil and cape. Sister Alice adds, "Her hand was extended. Her right hand moved gently to Her Heart as if she was beckoning the girl to come into her Heart. The girl turned to her mum and dad and saw the sun spinning, in different colours. Then the sun divided into four equal parts. Those parts joined together and formed one big heart. It was so red, and started pulsating like a human heart."

That September, the same girl was at the Fourteenth Station when the Virgin Mary appeared. The girl offered Mary a carnation. People standing nearby witnessed the carnation floating in the air.

In 1993, a natural spring on Shelagh and John's property became the focus of much attention. John had always used the spring to water his animals. Sister Alice explains, "At the time John had a troublesome growth on the third finger of his left hand which bled considerably. With his doctor's prescription he applied all kinds of medication to the growth but to no avail. He was scheduled for day surgery on his finger. One Saturday in early May, Josie suggested, 'Put your hand in the spring water.' He did so. That evening at Mass, John realized that the growth was gone, and believed the Blessed Mother had healed him."

On May of 1993, Dory Tan saw the Virgin Mary, who stated to her, "Make the water available. Tell the people to go to the water with strong faith and they will be healed."

This holy water has healed many people since then. A religious Sister from Kingston, Ontario, came to the farm for healing. She had an inoperable cyst on her pancreas. She drank the water. Four weeks later she returned exclaiming, "I haven't had as much as an aspirin since I drank the water here."

A thirty-year-old wife and mother was healed of life-long eczema on her hands, elbows, and arms by the holy water from the spring. She rubbed the water on the eczema and in only a few days it disappeared for good.

One common phenomenon at the farm is the scent of roses. Someone once described the smell as "strong and sweet and like the smell of a wet rose." Sister Alice highlights this oddity, "Sally and Roberto Bautista from Hamilton, Ontario, came to Marmora two and three times a year. On October 29, 1993, they drove a van with about twelve visitors from New Jersey, United States. They prayerfully made the Way of the Cross together. When they reached the Twelfth Station, the entire group saw the sun spinning, with a variety of colours. At the foot of the large cross they smelled the scent of roses. At this moment, Sally saw the image of the Blessed Mother. Sally felt heat on her face,

Decorative offerings at Stations of the Cross

and felt the rays of Our Lady's Face shining on her. Sally felt palpitations and heat all over her body. Then Our Blessed Mother raised her hands and blessed the whole group."

Father Frank Cox, Rector of St. Peter-In-Chains Cathedral in Peterborough, Ontario, calls Marmora a "Place of Pilgrimage and Prayer." He adds, "On more than one occasion I have experienced the fragrance of roses, like sweet, spicy old-country roses. This happened once while I was crossing an open meadow. The other occasion was while standing in conversation with another person at the garage. We both confirmed the rose scent which, like a blessed intimate whisper, was too soon gone, and yet not really."

My wife Allanah and my good friend Ron Mossop, who had worked as a missionary in the Hudson Bay district in the 1950s, drove with me from Parry Sound, Ontario, to Marmora to see for ourselves these miracles that happened at Greensides' Farm. An earlier telephone conversation with Sister Alice to arrange a meeting time at the Greensides' ended with her statement, "I know you will have an experience there."

While researching the Virgin Mary, I recalled watching a movie entitled *Our Lady of Fatima* sometime in the 1960s. The film was about the Blessed Mary appearing six times to three shepherd children, near the town of Fatima, Portugal, between May 13 and October 13, 1917. She came at a time when mankind was torn asunder by war and violence. She promised peace to the entire world if her request for prayer, reparation, and consecration were heard and obeyed. Was this happening again, first at Medjugorje, and now in Marmora, Ontario?

There was something else that seemed too much of a coincidence to me concerning the young boy, by the name of Karl Clemens, living on a family farm about two kilometres east of the village of Marmora, who went to see a film playing in the village. The film, *Our Lady of Fatima* had a powerful affect on Karl. Afterwards he climbed to the top of the hill at the back of the farm, and spoke to the Blessed Mother, "You did it there, why don't you do it here too, so that people can get to know you better?"

Karl grew up and left the farm. After some years in the teaching profession, Karl became a priest. The family farm was sold, and in 1972 was purchased by Shelagh and John Greensides. Twenty years later, the Blessed Mother came, answering young Karl's prayers.

Driving just east of Marmora, we saw the sign on the right side of the highway. It read GREENSIDES' LANE. We proceeded down the laneway until we reached two sizable parking lots lined with commercial buses and cars. From a distance I could see the farmhouse, the barn, and a few other buildings nestled at the bottom of a large hill. To my amazement, hundreds of people dotted the hillside and buses half-filled one parking lot. John Greensides welcomed us at the door with a warm smile. Shelagh was just inside the kitchen and greeted us with open arms. Now in their seventies, the Greensideses were happy and even excited to share their stories and their home. John remarked, "We have turned our farm over to the people and to worship. They come from all over the world, India, Hong Kong, England, Scotland, and Wales. We never advertise. People of all religious orders visit us; be it Catholics, Protestants, Buddhist, Muslims, or Ba'hi."

Shelagh added, "Anyone who comes to the door is welcome. We are open seven days a week. There are a lot of troubled people out there. They need a place to come to, to forget about their worries. People suddenly become boosted here."

The Greensideses shared a number of newspaper articles and testimonies with us before we departed to explore and experience the grounds.

I chose to begin with interviews, while Allanah and Ron proceeded through the Fourteen Stations. There were people everywhere, eating their lunch, sharing prayers in the prayer room next to the farmhouse, standing in small circles and singing, walking the pathway, evening lying on the ground. You couldn't help but feel peace in the vicinity of hundreds of people saying prayers. Sister Alice Johnson was one person I really wanted to meet. She is considered to be an expert in Marian-related phenomena and is a leading spokesperson with regards to supernatural events at Greensides' Farm in Marmora. It wasn't long before John came to get me.

Sister Alice and I talked at the kitchen table. I expressed my appreciation for her three books written about Marian-related phenomena. We spoke of spirits and of energy. Her time was short. We continued our conversation on route to her car. At that point she said to me, "You have a number of questions on the tip of your tongue, but you don't know which one to ask."

She was right.

Time to walk the Stations of the Cross; I had walked perhaps five steps along the path when suddenly I was struck by the smell of roses. I was amazed. It was right here that Father Cox had experienced the scent of roses and described it as "blessed intimate whisper." Next I caught sight of a young priest, Father Allan MacDonald of Cornwall, Ontario. I asked him if he believed that the Blessed Mother was appearing here. He replied, "I am here to honour what is happening."

At the First Station (where Jesus is condemned to death) I encountered people kneeling in prayer. Most people had rosaries in their hands. I passed more stations and saw many people praying. As I approached the Seventh Station (where Jesus falls a second time) I picked up the scent of roses again. With only artificial roses at that station I began to wonder if the Blessed Mary might appear at any moment.

Many relics, including flowers and pictures, were placed at the various stations.

One man's reason for his visit was very simply put, "When I leave here I feel better than when I first arrived. It is all about faith."

There were so many frail people praying for miracles of healing. Only faith could carry their tired bodies up that hill. Miracles have been recounted there.

Busloads of pilgrims on a daily basis

Pilgrims often pray for miracles

Lineup at spring with healing water. (I am in the line.)

Near the Fourteenth Station is the holy spring where people stand in long lines waiting for a drink of holy water. It was here that I saw Dory Tan speaking to a group of followers. Her presence certainly commands adoration. She can hear the Blessed Mother speaking. Could the Virgin Mary be there in front of me?

My visit had come to a close. Ron, Allanah, and I made our way to the car. During dinner we shared our experiences from the day. I told them of my experience of smelling roses. This had also happened to Allanah and Ron. In fact, Ron had also had his experience at the Seventh Station. As we headed through the Haliburton Highlands we felt energized and uplifted. It had been a sacred day for all of us. The setting sun marked our destination. As we each recalled our day a brilliant light flashed from a hillside in the distance. We looked at one another and we knew.

The Proctor House Museum

~ Brighton, Ontario ~

WHEN JOHN E. PROCTOR CLAIMED THE CORPSE OF JOHN NIX JUNIOR TO cover an unpaid debt, he set in motion a series of hauntings that continue to this day.

The Proctor house sits on a ninety-five-acre park-like setting originally owned by John Nix Senior. Nix Senior died in 1853 and the property was purchased by Isaac Proctor.

Bonnie Browne, author of *Brighton's Monument to Past Generations* states, "We believe Isaac [Proctor] had earned a great deal of money selling timber to England during the Crimean War. Isaac and his brothers, Pelltiah and John E., built the house [in stages] between 1853 and 1869. It is believed that the back portion of the brick saltbox construction was built first. The main section of the house containing the parlour, the morning room, the drawing room, the library, the upper hall, the widow's walk, and the family bedrooms was built later.

"Pelltiah, a doctor, had an office off the kitchen [door with frosted glass]. He suffered a heart attack in the house and died in 1860. Isaac died in 1866. John, his wife and five children moved into the house after the death of Isaac. He had accumulated some substantial revenue during the American Civil War and proceeded to begin construction on the new front portion of the house. The house and surrounding lands were originally called Millbank.

In the book entitled, *The Way We Were: Brighton Memories*, the authors stated, "The Italiante style of the house, complete with bay windows, brackets, servants' quarters and chandeliers, portrayed John E. Proctor as a man of means."

The first reported encounter with the paranormal was in 1900. During this time there were many sightings of a fiery ball in the immediate vicinity of the Proctor House. The fire ball has been written about extensively through the years, but never explained nor disproved conclusively.

Several stories vary, but many refer to the ball of fire as the ghost of John Nix Junior, haunting John Proctor's residence, as payback for some financial shenanigans. Other stories state the phenomenon is luminous methane phosphorus gas from a nearby millpond. Or was it, according to another story, just some local children flying a kite with a lamp as a prank.

The Proctor House, built between 1853–1869

The story of John Nix Junior begins in 1897. John Proctor held a mortgage on Nix's homestead. When Nix Junior fell ill, John Proctor visited Nix and ordered him to pay his debt before he died or he, John Proctor, would take Nix's body and sell it to medical science. Apparently Nix Junior responded to Proctor with "I will haunt you for the rest of your life if you take my body."

He died shortly thereafter; John Proctor and his brother, the sheriff, arrived at the home of Nix and removed the body. The body was then taken to the Proctor House and placed in the basement. Eventually the debt was paid and the family retrieved the body. They buried John Nix Junior in the Mount Hope Cemetery, just a two-kilometre drive from the Proctor estate.

In 1900, a fiery ball was sighted circling around the Proctor House. The fiery ball was considered to be the revenge of John Nix Junior on John Proctor. Some residents even swore they saw the ghost of Nix Junior in the ball of fire.

According to Bonnie Browne, "One Proctor relative, Mrs. MacDonald, tells of coming to Millbank as a child and listening to the ghost all night.

"Of course, there were many sounds in such a large house. Was it really the ghost or just a vivid imagination?

"Although these stories are part of Brighton's folklore we do not want these stories to keep you away. There have been no known sightings of the 'fire-ball' in more than eighty years."

An article published in the *Belleville Intelligencer* in 1988 stated, "The Brighton Proctor ghost has been unmasked." This is in reference to the ghost of John Nix Junior and the fire ball. "Allan Dempsey, a seventy-five-year-old Rednersville resident said Wednesday there is no ghost [Nix]. It's the product of active imagination and a boyish prank. 'Oh, I'll admit the other makes a better story.' The prank came to light when his father, William Charles Dempsey, visited his uncle Charles Drury in Brighton. "William, a curious boy at the time, saw this contraption out in the drive house. It was a kite with a light on it and his uncle Charles said the Drury boys used to fly it along the fence line at Proctor House on clear nights as a prank. People who saw the dancing light believed it was the ghost of a man who had vowed to return after death because Mr. Proctor had harassed his wife for debts owed when he died."

"In fact, said Dempsey, the story of Mr. Proctor seizing the man's body when he died until the debts were paid was true. The Drury boys ran their lighted kite from the unfortunate man's grave and along the fence line to the Proctor House."

Whether it was imagination, or the sight of a kite with a light dancing in the night, is still unknown, and despite the testimony of Allan Dempsey, the paranormal activity outside and inside the home continues to occur.

From the summer of 1991 to February 1992, the Fire Department and Harvey Davies, who was in charge of the maintenance of Proctor House, had many unexpected trips to the house. The smoke alarms and the security alarms seemed to go off continually — for no apparent reason.

Bonnie Browne stated, "The alarm manufacturers were called to check out the equipment but nothing was found to be out of order. In February 1992, it was determined that the newly installed gas furnace may have set off the smoke alarm, but what was setting off the burglar alarm?

"Later, when new insulation was installed in the attic, a worker found some frayed wires. Traps were placed in the attic area. Eventually six racoons were trapped. For days people had been talking about ghosts and many wondered if the mystery was solved."

Alarm system and smoke detector problems are common occurrences in settings known to be occupied by spirits.

The Proctor House today is a beautifully presented museum, maintained in its glory as it was created by the Proctor family. When the last owner passed on and no family members remained in Brighton, the town approached the family and it was donated to the town in 1976.

The original barn was not able to be restored, but Rene and Gerald Simpson donated a hundred-year-old barn from their property in 2000 and in 2001 the Proctor-Simpson Barn was opened as a theatre.

The Proctor House has some unusual features compared to others built at that time. Most builders used horsehair to bind and strengthen plaster but the Proctor family used the hair from their prized herd of purebred cattle; pine was used in most of the interior construction of the home, but grained to resemble oak.

According to Bonnie Browne, "The front doors and banister are made of oak. There is a circular stairway that was probably added after the original construction was completed. It is made of sawn lath and covers parts of the original door frames. It is believed that the Proctors saw circular staircases on a trip south and came home and remodelled the house to accommodate this feature."

The front doors of the Proctor House open to a long centre hall that extends to the kitchen. Red glass over the doorway was called "flash glass." A cylinder of clear glass was plunged into a vat of molten red glass, hence flash glass. The coloured glass produces a reflection in the sunlight that dances in the hallway.

On the immediate left there is a parlour, reserved for special occasions. The wallpaper is a reproduction of a 1777 Indian silk screen. The pillows in the room are hand-painted.

To the right is the morning room; it was the centre of family activities. The only fireplace in the house is situated in this room. At the time of construction an owner was taxed for every fireplace. Connected to the morning room is the dining room.

The hall doors are unique; made in the "pocket door" style — they slide and fold back, turning the entire area into a room large enough for a grand ball. In the hallway immediately beyond the parlour is the library, and Dr. Pelltiah Proctor's office. The kitchen at the end has a doorway to the basement, the summer kitchen, and the woodshed.

A back staircase from the kitchen leads up to the nanny's room on the second floor; there is a small adjoining room that served as the nursery. Three more steps complete the ascent to the main second-floor hallway. There is a small bedroom to the left and another narrow staircase that leads to the belvedere (widow's walk). In the hallway is the gallery to the right. At one time two bedrooms were housed in this area but it was opened up to create a museum/meeting room.

At the end of the hall on the left is the master bedroom. It is interesting to note that the upstairs hallway was once used as a sewing and sitting room by the family.

Perhaps the sheer beauty of this home held the Proctors captive after death.

A few years ago a group of people belonging to the Paranormal Seekers came to the home. The Paranormal Seekers are a scientifically based paranormal research and investigation group based in Durham Region, Oshawa.

From their website, "Does the Proctor House have a ghost? Yes. In fact, they have more than one, not only roaming around the house, but the grounds, as well."

The group was fortunate to spend an evening touring the house. Their tour guides for the evening were Ray and Anna Rittwage. The investigative team were made up of Brenda, Rachel, Jay, and Mike.

Also from the website, "As soon as Brenda walked in, she knew there was paranormal activity. Rachel and Brenda stood next to the long wooden kitchen table listening to Ray tell the history of the Proctor's home and family.

"Anna led Jay and Mike in further with the camera equipment. While the two girls were listening to Ray, one of the kitchen chairs had pulled out on its own, right into the back of Brenda. She felt as if someone was trying to sit at the table and she was in their way. Brenda also sensed that someone had somehow broken or crushed their right foot. They were pacing constantly back and forth along the side of the kitchen next to the cellar door."

The group continued on to the parlour room. They failed to see any spirits on the main floor, but sensed their presences. Brenda felt the visitation of a woman.

Central hallway where Dr. Pelltiah Proctor died of a heart attack. This is where Brenda, of the Paranormal Seekers, felt a cold spot

"We continued into the front hallway. As Brenda stood in the middle of the hall, she could feel her blood turning as cold as ice, as if she had died — a cold spot in the house."

According to tour guide Hannah Rittwage, Dr. Pelltiah Proctor died, on that spot, of a heart attack.

"From the morning room door, Brenda could sense a presence at the staircase and once into the morning room, Brenda could hear whispering, but was unable to make out the words. She felt anger in this room and could smell something sweet and bitter, perhaps imported cigars.

"Our tour Anna, noticed that the eyeglasses had been moved from the morning room to the table under the mirror in the hallway."

The group then climbed the main staircase to the second floor. Brenda could feel activity here and it seemed as though the higher they went the more intense the experience.

"On her way up the stairs, Brenda started to have various bladder pains and had to race to the nearest facilities.

"The group went next to the nanny's small bedroom. It was here that Brenda saw three girls, and Ray, the tour guide, told this story. 'One morning they entered the room and found a blanket on the floor at the foot of the bed. Unknown to them or other staff members was how it had arrived there.'

The kitchen where one female heard someone walking upstairs. She was alone in the building at the time

"At that moment the Paranormal Seekers heard a girl's voice state defensively, 'We had to cover the body. That is why we moved it.' The voice came from beside Brenda."

From the nanny's room they walked through a small doorway and into the adjacent bedroom.

"We started in a room to the left of the hall, which could have been one of the daughters' rooms. Brenda was drawn to the closet. She felt as though someone was inside the closet, but we found no one."

They still sensed someone was in the room with them. They were being watched! The group crossed the hall and entered the gallery.

"Brenda was afraid to open the closet in this room after feeling heat from behind the door. She could see someone who had broken his or her neck."

(We were informed that someone on the homestead had indeed done so. The body had been laid out in this very room.)

"Brenda stopped at the window that overlooked the front lawn, and placed her right hand on the pane of glass to peer out. She could feel a woman's hand where she had placed hers, also peering outside and waiting for something. She was innocent with thoughts, but was sad."

Leaving the gallery, they entered the master bedroom. Brenda caught sight of John Proctor pacing back and forth.

"We were then shown to a tiny set of stairs that leads up to the belvedere. We could feel great sorrow from an elderly woman. Brenda wanted to cry and felt it was hard to breathe."

It is said that John Proctor would climb up to the belvedere to keep a close watch on his many ships entering and leaving the Brighton Harbour.

Rose Ellery conducts ghost walk tours at the Proctor House. She has been doing this for several years. She shared a number of stories, beginning with this tale. "A twelve- or thirteen-year-old shot a picture of a raised, tanned leg wearing no socks, at the bottom of the stairs leading to the Belvedere."

Rose talked about the morning room. "Prior to the completion of the barn theatre the actors would use the morning room. In 1998, a group of actors were participating in a group photograph in front of the fireplace. A small blob was captured on film floating above the shoulder of one of the actors."

The morning room in the Proctor House. A small blob was photographed by the fireplace.

Rose had a personal experience in 2012. She was in the kitchen dealing with a call about ticket sales and she was alone in the building at the time.

"Late in the afternoon I heard footsteps above my head, which would have been in the nanny's room, in the old part of the house. A few minutes later I heard the slamming of the buffet cupboard door in the dining room by the stairs on the main floor. Somebody was so angry — just slamming the door. I still remained in the building.

"A few minutes later, Anna Rittwage, curator of the museum, arrived to close up. I told her what had just happened. We went into the dining room, but nothing had been disturbed.

"Last year I was upstairs in the house with a group of four people. Nothing unusual happened. Then the group asked if they could go outside to take some pictures. We were happy to oblige.

"The visitors went to the west side of the building and took a picture of the upstairs gallery. There are three large windows in the gallery. The visitors were astonished upon studying the photograph they had taken."

Rose explains, "In the middle window three people appeared, standing and looking out the window. One lad in the picture had a high neck and was wearing a sailor type hat, like they wore in the olden days. The man was wearing a top hat. The other person was not as distinctive and appeared to be smaller in stature.

"The visitors were really excited. We never thought to ask for a copy of the photograph."

Rose continued talking about the steep steps from the second floor to the belvedere. "A number of years ago, in June, we had a grade-three school group tour the building. The group climbed the stairs to the belvedere. Stash Connelly, the owner of the local paper, was there. She took my picture standing at the bottom of the stairs. To her surprise the photograph showed this thick white fog around my knees and all the way to the floor."

Rose referred to another similar occurrence, "One day a mother and daughter and a young man took the museum tour. The male visitor had a camera with him. He decided to go up the staircase to the belvedere to take some pictures of the scenery. Instead, he captured on film a heavy, white mass in the air."

Rose recalled the young boy who had taken the picture of a raised tanned leg by the stairs to the belvedere. "That young boy managed to shoot another picture. This time in the right-hand corner of the photograph the face of a soldier appeared, wearing a pith helmet. It was not a clear picture, but the person could have been in one of the Great Wars. It could have been a Proctor."

In the early 1990s, Tom Cunningham, president of Save Our Heritage Organization, would work in the back of the house on his computer. His dog, Scout, would come to work with him.

Rose added, "His dog would go up the back staircase leading to the nanny's room from the kitchen. When the dog would reach the nanny's room he would stop and bark in the direction of the three steps. He would not proceed any further.

"A few years ago, a female volunteer was working at the kitchen table, cataloguing some information, when she suddenly heard someone walking upstairs above the kitchen. This time the sound of footsteps lasted longer than the ones I heard. The volunteer was alone in the building at the time."

Rose finished the interview with a story about the nanny's room. "The nanny's room is decorated with braided rugs and an old rope bed with a straw-filled canvas cover. The linen press in the room is original to the house. An old-fashioned, white nightgown is laid out on the bed. During one tour the nightgown was discovered lying on the floor." Who had moved it and why?

Tour guides Hannah Rittwage and Emma Peters worked at the Proctor House during the most recent season, in 2013. Neither of the girls denies the existence of spirits roaming the house. Hannah is a firm believer in the possibility of spirits amongst us. On the other hand, Emma prefers to ignore their existence. In her words, "I tend to divert my eyes from any spirit activity in order to minimize the number of experiences."

In the summer of 2011, Hannah had quite an extraordinary experience on the second floor of the house. She caught sight of something or someone.

"I was upstairs in the small bedroom. I was looking at the mirror and caught sight of the reflection of a black figure moving out of the room.

The bedroom where Hannah Rittwage caught sight of the reflection of a black figure moving out of the room

"I was creeped out — terrified! I was never going to enter that room again. And I have never been back."

Emma likes to rationalize everything pertaining to the haunting. She believes it to be a safer way to work in a museum reputed to be haunted. She does have experiences, but remains unmoved.

For example, "I hear footsteps!

"One morning, I arrived at work and went upstairs to open the windows. I heard children laughing. I like to believe they were children outside of the museum!"

Emma reminds me that it is an old house that creaks and groans.

On another occasion Emma was on the phone speaking to a woman about taking wedding pictures at the Proctor House. Something bizarre happened to change the telephone conversation.

"Suddenly I heard a male voice yelling on the phone. I couldn't understand what he was saying. I asked the woman I had been speaking with, 'Is that your husband?' The woman replied, 'I didn't hear anything.'"

Emma did describe other peoples' encounters there.

"One child was visiting the house with his family. He reported hearing footsteps running downstairs and the front door opening and closing. The child fled the building.

"Apparently three little girls hang out in the backroom. A visiting psychic said the girls were connected to the donated toys. No little girls have ever died in the house.

"A visitor taking a photograph of the front doorway managed to capture the image of a little girl wearing a Victorian dress in the large window above the main door."

In August of 2013, Emma was walking through the nanny's room and discovered something unusual in the nursery that adjoins the room. In the nursery is a set of old, wooden bowling pins and other children's items.

"I always glance in at the nursery. To my amazement I saw that the bowling pins had been knocked over and the yellow and red balls had rolled over to where the baby carriage is situated. I reset the pins and balls and carried on with my day.

"Last summer [2012], I was walking about the house doing a usual routine for me. As usual, various objects had been moved during the night. In the nanny's room I found the white nightgown all scrunched up at the end of the bed. It is never like this."

There is a washroom situated in the hallway by the nanny's room. Emma mentioned another paranormal experience in this area of the house.

"A volunteer had gone to the washroom. After washing her hands she turned to get a paper towel. She turned back to shut the sink taps off. They had already been turned off."

Emma, herself, had an experience one day when she was about to close the museum.

"I was about to go to the belvedere when I caught sight of a wispy outline." (We cannot always maintain denial.)

The nursery where Emma Peters discovered the bowling pins knocked over.

The last Proctor family members to live in the home were Helena and Stella. They were spinster sisters. The ladies were the daughters of John E. Proctor. Helena died in 1930 and Stella in 1960. In 1970, the property was donated by John W. Proctor and the remaining heirs, to the people of Brighton. After a great effort by the citizens of Brighton and area the house was restored and opened as a museum on June 30, 1976.

Even though John Nix Junior was finally laid to rest, it would seem that some members of the Proctor family were not, and continue to walk the halls and rooms of the home they cherished. Perhaps you may be fortunate to meet one of the Proctors on your next visit to the museum.

The Port Perry Town Hall

~ Port Perry, Ontario ~

IT IS LATE IN THE EVENING; YOU ARE ALONE IN THE CENTURY-OLD building known as the Port Perry Town Hall. You hear footsteps. You call out, "hello." No one answers. But the lights go out. Uncertain now of your environment, fear pushes you instantly into a very different reality — the spirit world! Welcome to the Port Perry Town Hall.

In February of 1872 the subject of building a town hall for the newly incorporated town of Port Perry was discussed at a council meeting. Reeve Joseph Bigelow, councillors Tate, Philippa, and Serton were appointed to obtain plans and a construction estimate for a suitable town hall.

Six months later, Port Perry council passed a by-law to debenture $10,000 to secure a fire engine for their fire hall and to construct a town hall.

The location selected for the town hall was on the southwest corner of Queen and Lilla Streets.

Benjamin Crandell sold the parcel of land to the town for $1000 and construction began in the summer of 1873.

The shell of the town hall was completed that year and the interior work started for the winter months.

In March the editor of the local newspaper, the *Observer*, reported, "We had the pleasure the other day of visiting our new town hall. The mason work is being done in a manner which would do credit to any of our cities and fairly established the reputation of Mr Wm. Spence, as one of our most skilled contractors.

"The ceiling is really handsome, surrounded by a fine cornice about six feet wide with some six to eight centre pieces. This hall will be no less an ornament to the village than a credit to the liberality, enterprise and intelligence of its inhabitants."

Yet, there was never an official opening of the town hall. Unfinished work was delayed by tradespeople. Even in its incomplete state, a concert was held there and church services were performed there. Reeve Bigelow went ahead with an election meeting, despite the following newspaper update. "Naked of bricks on its lofty walls, had gaping joists and was in general incomplete state."

Despite the setbacks, the town hall served the needs of the community for nearly a century. Originally the township office, the building has also served as a jail (one holding cell), a theatre, a roller skating rink, a movie house, a fire station, and a ladies undergarment factory. Perhaps the varied activities in the building have led to the paranormal activity occurring there today.

In 1967, the town of Port Perry discussed the possibility of tearing down the town hall. Diane Lackie was one of seventeen people, many of whom were teachers, who organized themselves to form a committee to save the historic building from demolition. Their vision was to form an Arts Centre in the old town hall. They called their organization the Borelian Community Theatre. The mission statement was to stage quality amateur theatre by presenting Canadian theatre work and contemporary classics. The name Borelian was derived from the village of Borelia, now a part of Port Perry.

To assure the town of their determination, the committee members were each asked to promise $1000 if the need should arise. Since 1971, the volunteer board of directors of the Borelians remains committed to excellence in theatre, producing classic and contemporary works that challenge, educate, and above all, entertain their audiences.

In 1976, the Scugog Choral Society was formed and partnered with the Borelians. The society promotes amateur artistic talent and provides entertainment to enrich the cultural life of the community through musical productions.

Originally the Borelian volunteers met once a week to organize and complete minor renovations to the building. Diane still recalls the early days and the feeling that she was never alone in the building. "On occasion I would arrive at the hall at two o'clock in the morning to play the grand piano in front of a phantom audience. It was a really spooky place. The building was not yet finished. I heard many weird noises. Just let your imagination wander regarding the history of the building. In the dark, playing the piano at night, you hear things. I sensed things around me." Although Diane never saw a spirit in the hall, there were others who did!

Interior entrance to the theatre in Port Perry's Town Hall.

To gain a proper perspective of the building, you need to enter the side door of the hall on the Lilla Street side. As you enter you can see the ticket wicket. If you proceed straight ahead you will reach the washrooms, once a jail area; if you turn right and climb a short set of stairs to a small hallway, you will be facing the original doorway to the town hall. From that door a beautiful set of curved stairs leads to the theatre proper. The centre aisle, now a sloped theatre aisle, was once flat for factory machines, and roller skates and other activities held in the space. To the direct right of the stage a fire exit, once an alternative side door, is visible. There is a balcony section, accessed to the right of the door into the theatre itself. This balcony also houses the sound and lighting booth.

In the spring of 2013, I met with some of the people who were known to have "experiences" in this hall.

In 1981 Dave Ellis was directing a play in the hall. One night, toward the end of the evening, he found himself alone in the theatre. He shut the lights off in the back of the theatre and, in the dark, walked towards the exit door by the stage, but something happened to Dave that changed him forever.

Left to right: Alissa Smith, Irwin Smith, Allanah Douglas, Dave Ellis and Diane Lackie in the theatre (see orbs floating in the air and up the aisle.) Plenty of spirits here.

"As I was about to open the door something made me turn around to face the theatre seating and back balcony. There, up in the balcony area, was a woman entirely illuminated. She looked like she was floating in the air. She was indifferent and yet looking in my direction. She was wearing a long, flowing, period dress out of the late 1800s."

I asked Dave if he could see her face.

He replied, "I would describe her as seeing her features like looking at a rippling effect in water. She was there. It was definite. I was out of there. I have never, never been alone in the hall since!"

Alissa and Irwin Smith of Port Perry also joined me that spring evening in the hall. The Smiths are a well known family in the community and area. Their farm is the site of the Ocala Winery, a fine wine establishment that has won numerous awards for their wines. Alissa is the current chair of the town hall board of directors. The board oversees the general operations and upkeep of the building and hall rentals. Irwin is a well respected concert pianist and piano tuner in the district.

Thirteen years ago, Irwin had his first paranormal experience in the town hall. It was noon and Irwin was the only person in the building.

"I was there to tune the piano. When I first arrived I turned the stage lights on. As I sat down at the piano the staircase lights at the back entrance of the theatre went off!

"I said 'Hello?' No answer. Everything always seems to emanate from the back of the theatre. I don't dismiss it.

"Two years later, I was alone in the building also at midday. Once again, I was there to tune the piano. I was halfway through tuning the piano. My head was tilted listening to the piano with my right ear. I was facing the back of the stage. While I was tuning I heard footsteps in the aisle leading to the centre stage. The steps became louder. Then I heard the footsteps going up the short staircase onto the stage.

"I shouted out, 'Hey, it's me; I am just tuning the piano.' I carried on.

"Now the person was standing on the stage by the piano. I rose up to see who it was. There was no one there.

"It has never happened again. Now, when I come into the theatre I shout out, 'It's just me Irwin. I am just here to tune the piano.'"

During an earlier telephone conversation with Diane, she had shared a story about one resident spirit thought to be in the building.

"The story is about a local fellow in the early days that operated a still — an apparatus used to distill liquid mixtures by heating to a boil and then cooling to condense the vapour. The device was often used to produce distilled beverages containing ethyl alcohol in the district. Apparently the still blew up and he was caught by the police and jailed in the cell in the town hall. The cell was located in the area where the present-day washrooms are located. It is said that he died in the cell."

Although there is no historical record to confirm this event, Stewart, owner of the Wee Tartan Shop in downtown Port Perry had quite an unusual experience in the former cell area of the town hall.

Original jail cell door now just on display.

Stewart said, "Several years ago, just after they had put a new washroom in the basement, I was directing a show in the building. At the end of the evening, I was checking all the lights and making sure all the doors were closed and locked.

"Before leaving, I saw the lights on in the gents' washroom and felt I should stop in there before heading home. I sat down and the door opened and a very cold breeze came into the cubicle. Then the lights went out. I called out as I thought I had missed someone who had not left, but no one answered and the door closed.

"I very quickly got up and turned the lights back on, wondering if the power had gone off or that a timer had been activated. I later enquired if there was such a timer and there was none.

"As you know, the basement area was once a jail cell in the old town hall and a few prisoners still haunt the place.

"I have had to close up several times in the past few years and although not scared, I usually try to make sure someone is with me. It is a very scary place at night."

The jail cell door is still in the building; leaning against the wall by the washroom area.

Before we ended our session that night in the town hall Alissa suddenly recalled another unexplained incident that had recently occurred.

"A spectator in the audience during a choral play swears they saw an unidentified person in the chorus performing up on stage. No one knows who it was!"

Irwin also recalled another unusual occurrence in the building.

"Three years ago, I was operating the sound system during a performance. During the first part of the play I could hear that the sound wasn't quite right. At intermission I examined the music board to see if there was a problem. To my surprise, the wires to the board had all been switched around. Someone or something had sabotaged the sound system!"

Who would have done such a thing?

Who enjoys sabotaging the sound system during a performance? Could it be a former actor who was shunned for a part in a play?

It would seem that someone who found themselves behind bars at the old Port Perry Town Hall never left. In regards to the theatre, one spirit still enjoys participating in a good stage show. Who was the woman watching Dave from above? She certainly wasn't afraid to show herself. Maybe she worked in the building when it was a ladies' undergarment factory.

Why does it seem to be a very scary place? Is it scary, or is it just in our mind? Either way, you might want someone to accompany you if you decide to visit the old Port Perry Town Hall; you never know what experience you may have there.

Herongate Barn Theatre
~ Whitevale, Ontario ~

ACTORS OCCASIONALLY BECOME QUITE ATTACHED TO A THEATRE. IN fact, after their demise they may just return to star in a leading role. Alas, only a very few people in the audience would ever hear or see them. Some actors may "come back" as part of an audience, or perhaps as a critic, to watch a performance. They could even return to mess with the technical equipment.

Interested in a theatrical encounter? Try Herongate Theatre.

Herongate was once a thriving, century-old dairy farm that later served as a location for auctions, barn dances, and hay rides. In 1975, Alban and Pat Ward conceived the idea of creating a home for live theatre in a rural setting and found the perfect setting on Altona Road near the community of Whitevale (north of Pickering).

The world of theatre is home to many superstitions and lore that needs to be given some attention. Most of us are familiar with the expression "break a leg" — saying it will prevent bad luck and injury, or so it is believed. Three candles burning at the same time on stage is bad luck. The person closest to the shortest candle will be the next to marry, or die.

Peacock feathers brought on stage, for any purpose, are also believed to bring chaos. Veteran thespians have stories to tell about sets collapsing and curtains catching fire during performances where peacock feathers were used on stage. The eye of the peacock feather is said to represent a malevolent "evil eye" that bestows a curse upon the show.

The custom of having a single light burning in an empty theatre to ward off ghosts became a precaution against negative influence and disruptions from the spirit world.

It is good luck to give the director and/or the leading lady a bouquet of flowers after the last performance.

A Toronto actor by the name of Donald Reid performed in a series of plays during the early years of Herongate. He starred in *The Owl and the Pussy Cat*, *The Mousetrap*, and *Butterflies are Free*. His stage name was Gemmel Reid.

Eventually Donald also played the leading role of Mortimer Brewster in the play, *Arsenic and Old Lace*, written by American playwright, Joseph Kesselring in 1939.

A brief outline of the play will provide appropriate context for this amazing, incredible tale of haunting.

In *Arsenic and Old Lace*, Mortimer falls in love and marries his childhood sweetheart from Brooklyn. When they visit his elderly spinster

A real barn – a real theatre!

aunts, Abby and Martha, and his brother, Teddy, Mortimer discovers murder. Initially he believes Teddy, who thinks he's Theodore Roosevelt and yells "charge!" when he climbs the stairs, to be the guilty party. In the end, however, his aunts take the credit — they were poisoning lonely bachelors to relieve them of their suffering, using elderberry wine spiked with arsenic, strychnine, and a pinch of cyanide.

Teddy buries the bodies in the basement, believing them to have died of the "yellow fever."

Donald Reid did not survive the play. How could that be? Such a dramatic end!

Ann Ward, the daughter of Alban and Pat, recalls the entire event. Ann was a young woman at the time — just beginning her career.

"Donald got the lead role in the play *Arsenic and Old Lace*. I was cast as the love interest, Elaine Harper. Donald was a slim, tall, handsome character. We got to know one another quite well.

"One night he was sitting with his girlfriend and another man. Apparently the man was also his lover."

"On this particular night we were in the wings of the stage. Donald didn't seem right. He was on his hands and knees asking me to help him.

Herongate Barn Theatre billboard.

He got up and went out on stage walking towards a hutch. He suddenly swung his arm and the hutch went over and crashed on the stage. That was the end of the act!"

Ann was only eighteen years of age at the time and had no idea of the steps Donald would take to manage, or to end, the anxiety he felt. One day Donald gifted Ann a brooch. She considered it a gesture of friendship.

Two days later Donald committed suicide.

Ann explained that Donald had a part-time job working in a laboratory. The night of his death he had consumed both arsenic and cyanide. It was more than a little ironic, considering his role in the play.

Ann believes Donald was probably struggling with his sexuality. After all, it was the 1970s and the majority of gay people were still very cautious of revealing their gender preferences.

Well, Donald died, but did he leave?

Ann adds, "Since Donald's death there have been numerous happenings when there is a play showing that Donald would have had a part in."

Shortly thereafter Ann went to California, where she studied theatre for the next ten years. During that time she heard many comments from her parents about things being "moved around" mysteriously.

Ann commented, "The activity increased after my return."

Herongate stage where numerous plays are staged each year.

"Once, when I was on stage rehearsing, all the lights went out. On another occasion, when I was closing everything down for the night, a candle flame ignited on a table in the restaurant. I immediately called out, 'Okay, Donald, if you appear in front of me I will drop dead.'

"I remember the energy being heavy and scary — the atmosphere was pulsing."

When she, herself, was directing *Arsenic and Old Lace*, she had another experience. "I was working on the set, hanging wallpaper. Suddenly I heard this loud crash in the balcony area. It sounded just like the time Donald knocked over the hutch."

During a subsequent performance of *Arsenic and Old Lace*, she had this experience. "At the end of the first act, the scene where Donald would have knocked over the hutch, actor Mike Woodbridge was pushed off the stage into the front row seats by unseen hands." If that wasn't enough, a tragic event happened a few years ago — tragic for Ann's partner, Steve Graham, and for the whole of Herongate.

One day Steve arrived at the theatre and found Jim Carey, their technical and lighting man, sitting in his car in the parking lot. Steve asked him if he was okay. Sadly, Jim was in severe medical distress and died in Steve's arms.

He was cremated and his ashes were buried on the Herongate grounds. He left a legacy. He has remained, in spirit, to oversee the technical needs of the theatre. It would seem that whenever Jim foresees electrical or lighting problems he gives Steve a sign, to draw his attention to the situation. For example, a bulb might flash on and off. Steve commented that on one occasion an electrical breaker flipped three times. Upon investigation, Steve invariably discovered an electrical problem in that area of the theatre.

Actors have seen someone moving about in the lighting booth when no one was in the booth.

It would seem that Jim's attached and still working, too!

Ann spoke of another unusual experience at Herongate.

A play was being staged entitled, *I'll be back before Midnight*. The play was about a husband who was driving his wife crazy, in order to be with his girlfriend.

The play has been described by the Toronto *Globe and Mail* as the most widely produced stage play in Canadian history. It has also been produced in twenty-nine countries. Here's the gist of it:

Jan has recently had a nervous breakdown and her husband, Greg, an archaeologist, has rented an old farmhouse in the country, where she can recover.

They rent the house from George, a hilarious farmer who tells stories about a murder that once took place in the rental farm. There is a ghost that reputedly stalks the night.

Jan's imagination gets fired up. There is some mention of blood and to dramatize this for the murder, they had an intravenous bag full of dish soap and food colouring.

Ann came to work one morning and discovered that the bag of "blood" had been dropped and had formed a large pool of liquid on the stage floor. Ann noticed immediately that footprints had appeared across the stage floor, as though someone had walked through the liquid. Someone, size eleven ... the same size as Donald's feet.

Once, Ann arranged a birthday party in the backroom of the restaurant. She had created loot bags, each containing twenty pieces of chocolate loonies and costume jewellery, for the birthday participants.

Ann set the bags out on the tables. The next morning, she discovered that the chocolate loonies were missing from every bag. The chocolate loonies never reappeared, but the wrappers did! The wrappers started to appear everywhere in the building, on chairs and tables. Every chocolate wrapper that went missing eventually turned up. Ann said, "Jim loved candy."

Peter Hurley, a professional actor, starred in theatrical roles at Herongate for eighteen years, beginning in 1981. Peter believes that the field of paranormal studies is, at this time, a philosophy of science.

He said, "We might psychologically create these scenarios. However, we really do not know. I do know we have verified experiences. We do not know what is going on. We have really good stories and lots of questions.

"I often hung out at the theatre after work. Actors would use the side door to enter the back stage of the theatre. One night I heard the screen door open and close shut. I called out, 'Hello'.

"No answer."

"I walked back, but no one was there. I went downstairs and asked the actors if anyone had come in. The answer was no."

During a later production of *Arsenic and Old Lace*, Peter encountered some other unusual activity.

"A suitcase moved from one side of the stage to the other without anyone's help. Props continued to be moved around, and we also experienced power outages."

Tim Moore, a set builder, had an unexplained experience in January of 2011.

"I was in the restaurant reading a script. Suddenly, I heard footsteps upstairs. It was like someone was walking around. Then the stage door slammed shut. I decided to go upstairs and have a look around. Nobody was there.

"I checked outside, but there were no cars in the parking lot. There was no one here!"

Herongate Theatre definitely has some folks attached and it would seem to be both actors and technicians. Whatever the spirit attachment is, it is interesting. Do come and try it.

The Keefer Mansion Inn

~ Thorold, Ontario ~

THE KEEFER MANSION INN IN THOROLD, ONTARIO, IS TRULY AN EXCEPtional bed and breakfast establishment, hosting weddings, family and corporate celebrations, and ghosts! It is not very often you can stay in one place and have a haunting experience in almost every room. You will never feel lonely here. There are plenty of spirits to lift your spirits. The question is, "Who is the company?"

I know the tales of spirit activity in the Keefer Mansion are true. I met one spirit there and I had witnesses!

The Keefer family was one of Canada's most important engineering dynasties. They directed the construction of railways, bridges, and water and sewage works. It was George Keefer who served as the first president of William Hamilton Merritt's Welland Canal Company. The Welland Canal is a ship canal that stretches from Port Weller on Lake Ontario to Port Colborne on Lake Erie. The canal was designed to enable ships to ascend and descend the Niagara Escarpment, and bypass Niagara Falls.

The family can trace their early roots to France and, later, to Germany. Their original name was Le Tonnellier (the Cooper). When they moved to Germany, the name changed to Keiffer (translated to Cooper) because the family owned a barrel making business that had been operated for generations.

In 1749, the family moved to what is now New Jersey, in the United States. Their name changed again to Keefer to ensure proper pronunciation. The Keefers remained loyal to the crown during the American Revolution. As a result, the family were forced to eventually flee the United States. By 1790, George, age seventeen, and his brother Jacob age fifteen, set out for Upper Canada to scout out a new place to live. In their travels they encountered a lone squatter, living in a small hut. The brothers reached an agreement with him and purchased the property. For the next two years they cleared the land and built a log home. Then they went back to New Jersey and returned with their families shortly thereafter. Upon their return George also acquired a land grant of six hundred acres, in the area soon to be named Thorold.

George would later practice land surveying and operate a general store in the community. He owned two sawmills and a grist mill. George and his wife, Catherine Lampman raised a very large family. In 1839, George deeded the property, then consisting of twenty-three acres, to his fourth son, John.

The Keefer Mansion Inn, 1886

By 1885, the original log home needed to be replaced. It was time to construct a dwelling that reflected the prosperity the Keefer family had acquired through their hard work and determination. The dwelling, named Maplehurst, was truly a unique structure of stone and wood. According to the Keefer Mansion Inn website, "The current mansion took just over a year to construct. When complete, it was reported to be 'one of the most splendid homes opened in 1886 between Toronto and Rochester'. Just the stone alone was reported to cost $30,000, in 1885. Notable features of the 9000-square-foot structure include; the new Harris hot water system, indoor plumbing, extensive wood details, ornate hardware, a tunnel to the canal, and an upper widow's walk."

The stone fence that surrounds the mansion cost an additional $5000. One source stated that the stone came from Europe. Another source reports that the red stone was from Griffith's quarry and the white cut stone came from Queenston, Ontario. What *is* known is that during the construction there were thirty-two stonemasons at work on the building.

Many of Thorold's history books list Hugh, one of John Keefer's sons, as the builder of Maplehurst. One source states that Hugh was quite a gambler and went to the United States where he accumulated much money at the tables. Hugh was also reputed to have been a frequent gambling partner of the notorious Jesse James; it is said he married Jesse's sister before returning to Thorold to construct Maplehurst. Maybe Jesse James returns to Maplehurst today in hopes of visiting his sister at a family gathering.

Unfortunately, the Keefers only enjoyed their estate for eight years — it was repossessed by the Permanent Loan and Savings Company in 1894. This demonstrated changing times and dwindling financial resources for John and Hugh Keefer.

Over the next few years, various tenants resided at Maplehurst. In 1934, the estate was purchased by Mary J. Brittain (a nurse) for $10,500. Mary and her family lived onsite while they converted the rooms to accommodate a maternity hospital. People often report hearing children during a stay there.

In 1936, Mary lost the place and her business due to a default on the mortgage. However, the superintendent of the hospital, Florence

Stevenson purchased the place, at a public auction, for only $3,500, plus municipal taxes. Under Florence's leadership the dwelling became a hospital for minor surgeries (tonsils and babies).

She ran Maplehurst Hospital along with her mother, and resided there until her sudden death at the age of forty-three, on July 9, 1950. The building and property was sold to Florence's mother, Mabel Stevenson. In 1953, Mabel sold the hospital to Helen Lohnes, a local nurse, and Marguerite Charron, a drug clerk. They operated the hospital for the next twenty years.

In 1973, Basil Griffis purchased Maplehurst Hospital. He ran the place as a chronic care hospital, housing patients from age twenty-eight to ninety-five.

Griffis decided to put in an application to expand the hospital. He wanted to add a three-storey addition to the property. He wanted to go into senior care. The process dragged out, and eventually the Ministry of Health refused his application, citing a surplus of nursing home beds in St. Catherines.

The chronic care hospital continued until March of 1999, when Mr. Griffis decided to sell. He could not find any buyers, so he applied for a demolition permit. Mayor Robin Davidson and the counsel of Thorold intervened and purchased the building.

In 2002, the City of Thorold entered into a long-term lease with Keefer Development Ltd. The president of Keefer Development is Phil Ritchie, who oversees the operations of the mansion today.

It was summer, early morning, when I drove up the driveway to the Keefer Mansion. I had heard stories about hauntings there, but had not visited before. The building is majestic, situated high on a hill, overlooking the Welland Canal.

The interior of the home is absolutely spectacular, with antique furniture and unusual lighting features. At the front desk I met a lovely couple, Nicole and Jason Sawatsky, who assist in the operations of the hotel. I explained who I was and that I was here to write a story about the Keefer Mansion and its reported hauntings. They were quite gracious and agreed to guide me through the building on a tour.

In the past eight years, several paranormal groups and mediums have visited the Keefer Mansion. One such medium was Gordon, a gifted seer who has visited the mansion and has captured a picture showing that someone had been sitting on the bed in room 201. The blanket was indented as though someone had been seated there. No one else had been in the room.

The Niagara Amateur Ghost Seekers have visited the place on four separate occasions. On one visit, one or two group members saw two figures in a window on the third floor, on the west-facing side of the mansion.

One figure was described as a young child and smaller than the other figure. The larger figure seemed bigger and appeared to be curious about the group below. A female presence was sensed on the main staircase. The spirit of a male soldier, quite possibly from the Second World War, was sensed on the second floor. One member of the group felt the spirit was "depressed and wondering about his fate."

In one room, on the second floor, someone could smell an odour. They described the smell as that of iodine. Had they tapped into the time when the house was a hospital, possibly true for the soldier, when chronically-ill patients were housed here?

One member of the Niagara Amateur Ghost Seekers felt the presence of a female child on the third floor. They received a message that her name was Anna. She was no more than eight years old.

Another incredible incident that occurred was the appearance of a child's palm print on one of the windows.

Nicole and Jason talked about whether or not the spirits liked them. They feel a very strong indication that they are liked and they find this place to be very healing. For example, Nicole has arthritis. There are times when she suffers incredible pain with no relief. She said, "As soon as I leave the house my knuckles seem to swell and my joints ache." By contrast, when she spends time in the mansion, she feels some relief from the pain. She finds the building "very healing for me."

Nicole, Jason, and I set out on our tour of the house. We climbed the central staircase to the second floor. The wooden doors to the rooms are very large, and heavy to open and close. Since almost every room in the establishment has a story, we started in room 202. We entered the room, closed the door, and sat down. I was just about to ask my first question when the door to the room flung open suddenly, and with an incredible force it slammed shut. The sound reverberated intensely. We all bolted upright, taken aback by this sudden disturbance. It was extreme, to say the least. What prompted that response?

I thought that Nicole and Jason might take this as an omen, a sign that I should not be doing an interview or a story about the place. However, it was the opposite response. They took it as a sign of affirmation that the spirits wanted to let me know they were around, an odd way to extend a welcome. We carried on.

Room 204 had been the birthing room in the hospital. One medium felt unsettled in her stomach, when she was in that room; conversely, some people feel uncomfortable.

Room 203 has a bed that is always warm. The sheets feel warm, as if someone had recently lain there. The presence living in this room has been identified as two sisters.

I felt quite uneasy after the slamming door experience in room 202. I looked around repeatedly to see if someone was there, and I was definitely staying out of doorways!

With no further incidents on the second floor, we proceeded to climb the stairs to the third floor. The third floor had been sealed off during the hospital days. There had been a time when this floor was the

The heavy door that slammed to declare the presence of the spirits.

ballroom. They told me that the window, at the top of the staircase to the third floor, opens on its own in the middle of the night. Here, on the third floor, people hear children's voices, and here the paranormal group saw a child in the window.

People who stay in room 303 experience a very welcoming energy. Room 304 has a fabulous view of the Welland Canal. The third floor also has a unique feature — a secret passageway. A bookcase swings open to reveal a secret staircase to the widow's walk. No stories were told but one can only wonder.

Nicole and Jason then led me to the basement, where they shared their own personal experience.

Secret staircase leading
to the widow's walk.

"One day all ten rooms were booked for a wedding. Jay [Jason] and I slept that night in the change room in the basement. As soon as my head hit the pillow I became sick. I had problems breathing, and I said 'Please leave me alone' [to the spirits]. At three o'clock in the morning, Jay heard something fly across the floor.

"I walked out of the change room and saw a bag of dried peppers on the floor. The peppers had been moved six feet across the floor, from where they had been stored."

People have claimed that there is paranormal activity on the grounds of the estate. They believe it might be a former groundskeeper of days gone by.

Maplehurst, or the Keefer Mansion Inn, as it is now called, is charming and alluring. Enchanting and mysterious are the words that I would use. It has had many transformations; people have lived here and died here. Love and caring still permeate the very walls of this dwelling. Of course, there could be some imprint of anger and despair from those chronic patients but, if so, it is minor.

People are attracted to the Keefer Mansion, and feel encompassed by the presence of the place. Adjectives often used are "fantastic," "child-friendly," "mysterious," and "romantic."

Another customer adds, "We had a chance to dine at the restaurant in the Keefer Mansion. This is definitely Niagara region's best kept secret. Dinner was excellent, with some great options as well as terrific specials.

"This place could do a wicked 'murder mystery night.'"

The Keefer Mansion Inn is definitely a setting where one might encounter a paranormal experience.

If you would like to visit

Black Creek Pioneer Village
1000 Murray Ross Parkway
Toronto, Ontario
416-736-1733
Website: www.blackcreek.ca
Email: bcpvinfo@trca.on.ca.

The Elgin and Winter Garden
Theatre
189 Yonge Street
Toronto, Ontario
416-314-2874
Website: www.heritagetrust.on.ca/
ewg
Email: ewg@heritagetrust.on.ca.

The Cawthra Estate
1507 Cawthra Road,
Mississauga, Ontario

905-615-4800
Cherry Hill House
680 Silver Creek Boulevard,
Mississauga, Ontario

The Blue Elephant
96 Norfolk Street South
Simcoe, Ontario
519-428-2886
Website: www.bluelephant.ca

Eldon House
481 Ridout Street North
London, Ontario
519-661-5169
Website: www.eldonhouse.ca
Email: info@eldonhouse.ca

Greystones Inn
63 Boradway Street
Orangeville, Ontario

Orillia Opera House
20 Mississauga Street West
Orillia, Ontario
705-326-8011
Website: www.orilliaoperahouse.ca

Greensides' Farm
103414 Highway 7
R.R. 2, P.O. Box 541
Marmora, Ontario
613-472-2560
Website: www.marmoraon.ca/
farm.html

Proctor House Museum
96 Young Street
Brighton, Ontario
1-613-475-2144
Website: www.proctorhouse
museum.ca
Email: info@proctorhouse
museum.ca

Herongate Barn Theatre
2885 Altona Road
Whitevale Ontario
905-472-3085
Website: www.herongate.com

The Keefer Mansion
14 St. David Street West
Thorold, Ontario
905-680-9581
Website: www.keefermansion.com

Bibliography

Books

Book Committee. *That's Just The Way We Were, Brighton Memories.* Brighton: Brighton History Book Committee, 2006.

Browne, Bonne. *Brighton's Monument To Past Generations.* Self's Printing, 2000.

Chambers, *Ghosts and Sprits.* Edinburgh: Chambers Harrap Publishers Ltd., 2008.

Colombo, John Robert. *Haunted Toronto.* Toronto: Hounslow Press, 1996.

Crow, Catherine. *The Ghosts of Black Creek.* Barrie, 2007.

Friends of St. Thomas Public Library. *Memories of St. Thomas and Elgin.* St. Thomas, 2000.

Harvey, Irwin, & Watt, Caroline. *An Introduction To Parapsychology,* North Carolina: McFarland and Company Inc., 2007.

Hick, Kathleen. *Clarkson and Its Many Corners.* Mississauga: Mississauga Library, 2003.

Holzer, Hans. *Ghosts.* New York: Aspera Ad Astra Inc., 1997.

Orillia Opera House Management Committee. *Phantoms of The Orillia Opera House*. Orillia, 1995.

Sonin, Eileen. *Ghosts I Have Known*, Toronto: Clarke, Irwin and Company Limited, 1960.

Sonin, Eileen. *Canadian Ghosts*. Toronto: Simon and Schuster of Canada Ltd, 1970.

Townsend, Wayne. *Orangeville*. Toronto: Natural Heritage Books, 2006.

Magazines

da Silva, Maria & Hind, Andrew. "Burnick House, Black Creek Pioneer Village." *Fate Magazine* (2005).

Index